The Maryland Adventure

Suzanne Ellery Chapelle

GIBBS·SMITH
PUBLISHER

SALT LAKE CITY

08 07 06 05 04 03 02   10 9 8 7 6 5 4 3

Published by
Gibbs Smith, Publisher
P.O. Box 667
Layton, Utah 84041

1-800-748-5439
text@gibbs-smith.com
www.gibbs-smith.com/textbooks

Managing Editor: Courtney Johnson Thomas
Associate Editors: Susan Myers, Amy Wagstaff, Jodi Sanford, Aimee Larsen
Book Design: Robert Holman
Picture Research: Jean Wittich
Research Assistant: Jennifer Greene
Cover Photo: *Pride of Baltimore II* by Bill McAllen

About the Author:
Dr. Suzanne Ellery Chapelle is a member of the History Department at Morgan State University in Baltimore. Her undergraduate degree is from Harvard University and her Ph.D. is from the Johns Hopkins University. She served as senior author and editor of *Maryland: A History of Its People*, a high school textbook published by the Johns Hopkins University Press in 1986. She worked on a revision of *A Child's History of the World*, published by the Calvert School, and contributed eight new chapters. She is also the author of *Baltimore: An Illustrated History*. She volunteers for the Marine Animal Rescue Program at the National Aquarium in Baltimore and gives nature education walks at the Irvine Natural Science Center.

Printed and bound in China
ISBN 0-87905-896-X

This book is dedicated to the students and teachers of Maryland. You are the future not only of our state, but of the world. Try to think as far as your heart and imagination will take you. Use the valuable lessons of our past to build a better future for all the world's people.

Contents

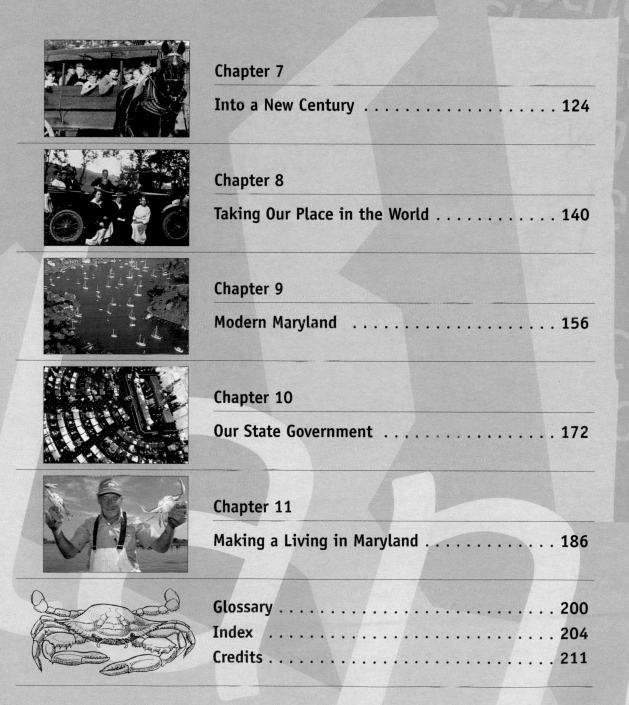

Maps

State Symbols

White Oak

Baltimore Oriole

Chesapeake Bay
Retriever

Checkerspot
Butterfly

Rockfish

Black-Eyed
Susan

Diamondback
Terrapin

State Flag

What symbols make up the pattern on Maryland's state flag? The gold and black design represents the Calvert family, who founded the Maryland colony. The red and white design represents the Crossland family. The mother of George Calvert, the first Lord Baltimore, belonged to the Crossland family.

State Seal

The governor and secretary of state use the state seal for official purposes and important government papers.

chapter 1

Natural Maryland

chapter 1

TERMS TO UNDERSTAND
geography
miniature
peninsula
glacier
tributary
temperate
drought
extinct
fossil
ancestor
migrate
native
fertile
dense
fall line
ecosystem
predator
endangered

A family of geese goes for a swim in Deep Creek Lake.
(Photo by Lance Bell, Courtesy of AAD, Inc.)

THE LAND WE CALL HOME

MARYLAND MAY SEEM very large to us. Yet it is just a small part of the world. Because we live in Maryland it is important to us. This is our home.

In this chapter we will begin to learn about Maryland by studying its *geography*. Geography is the study of the land, water, plants, animals, and people of a place. First we will learn where Maryland is located in the world. We will study Maryland's land and waterways. We will see how plants, animals, and people live here. We will see the connections between us and the world around us.

Why is it important to know about geography? Geography affects where and how we live. For example, more people live on flat land than in the mountains. Flat land is easier to farm. It is easier to build houses on flat land. Many people live near water. They use the rivers, bays, and ocean for transportation. People, animals, and plants all need water to survive. Our land and our water are very important to us.

Do you live in farm country or in a big city?

Where in the World Are We?

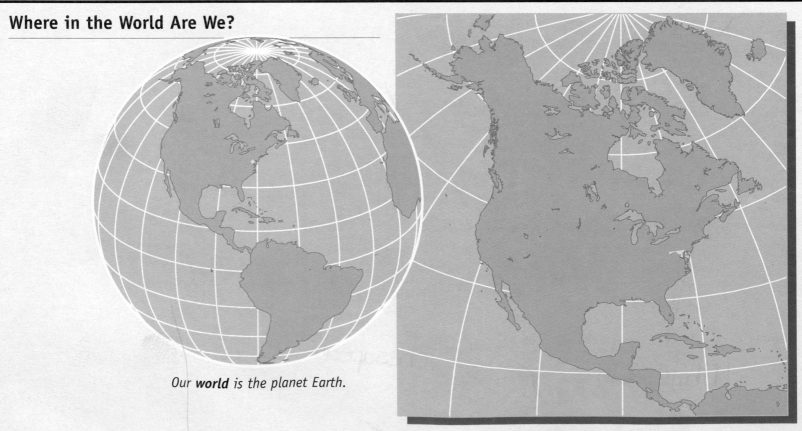

*Our **world** is the planet Earth.*

*Our **continent** is North America.*

LOCATION

We all know we live on the planet Earth. What else do we know about where we live? Maryland is located on the **continent** of North America. Continents are very large land areas. They have oceans or seas on many sides. Which oceans touch North America?

Maryland is part of the **country** of the United States of America. A country is a land region under the control of one government. The country to our north is Canada. The country to our south is Mexico. Can you find these countries on a map?

Our country is divided into **states**. Maryland is one of fifty states. Maryland is on the East Coast of the United States. It lies next to the Atlantic Ocean. Our neighboring states are Delaware, Pennsylvania, West Virginia, and Virginia. Our nation's capital, Washington, D.C., also borders Maryland. Can you find all these places on a map?

States are divided into **counties**. Within each county there are cities, towns, neighborhoods, and farms.

Solar System
Planet
Continent
Country
State
County
City or Town
Neighborhood or Farm

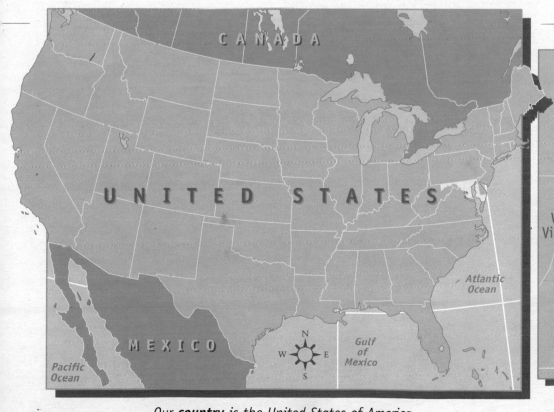

*Our **country** is the United States of America.*

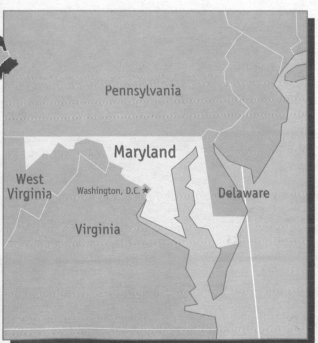

*Our **state** is Maryland.*

Lighthouses flash bright lights to help sailors know their location when it is too dark or too foggy to see. Which features shown here are natural? Which are man-made?

PLACE

What kind of place is Maryland? All places have certain features that make them alike or different from other places. Some of these features are natural to the environment, such as animals, plants, soil, mountains, rivers, bays, and oceans.

Places also have human features. There are cities, farms, homes, roads, bridges, and shopping malls. These are things that people have made. These things change the natural environment.

America in Miniature

Maryland is often called "America in *miniature*." Why do you suppose people say this? If you guessed that it's because Maryland is like a small-sized version of America, you are right.

Our small state is called "America in miniature" because it has so many of the natural and human features that we see all across our country. We have beaches and wetlands, cities and industries, mountains and mines. Forests, farms, and towns stretch

Maryland is the eighth smallest state in the country. That means only seven states are smaller. Can you list them?

The Maryland Adventure

across our state. Small streams flow into our big rivers and, from there, into the Chesapeake Bay. We do not have great wide plains or deserts like those in the West, but we certainly have a lot of variety in one small place.

A Place with Lots of Water

Maryland is next to the Atlantic Ocean. It also has the Chesapeake Bay. The bay's shoreline is long and curvy. The land on the eastern side of the bay is called the Eastern Shore. The land west of the bay is called the Western Shore.

The Eastern Shore is part of a large *peninsula*. It is called the Delmarva Peninsula. A peninsula is an area of land surrounded by water on three sides. Find the Delmarva Peninsula on the map.

The Potomac River is our largest river. Maryland has many other rivers, such as the Susquehanna, Gunpowder, and Patapsco Rivers. Most of our rivers flow into the Chesapeake Bay.

Maryland does not have many lakes. Deep Creek Lake is the largest. It is a man-made lake.

Do you know how the Delmarva Peninsula got its name? It includes parts of three states: De_la_ware + _Mar_yland + _Va_irginia = Del-mar-va.

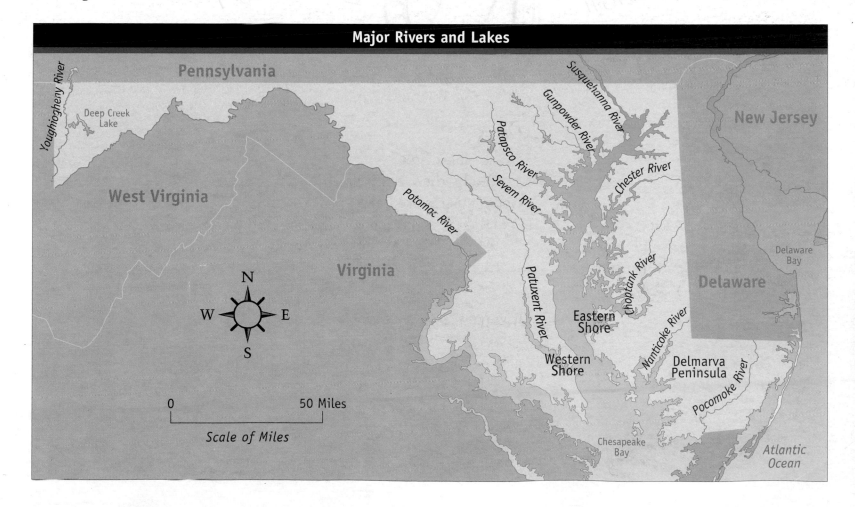

Major Rivers and Lakes

Pennsylvania

Youghiogheny River

Deep Creek Lake

West Virginia

Patapsco River

Gunpowder River

Susquehanna River

New Jersey

Severn River

Chester River

Potomac River

Virginia

Patuxent River

Choptank River

Nanticoke River

Delaware Bay

Delaware

N
W   E
S

Eastern Shore

Western Shore

Delmarva Peninsula

Pocomoke River

0   50 Miles

Scale of Miles

Chesapeake Bay

Atlantic Ocean

Chesapeake Bay

THE CHESAPEAKE BAY is one of our country's most valuable treasures. If you have seen the bay, you know that it is very beautiful. It is also important in many ways. A lot of people earn their living at jobs that depend on the bay. Many plants and animals also depend on the Chesapeake Bay.

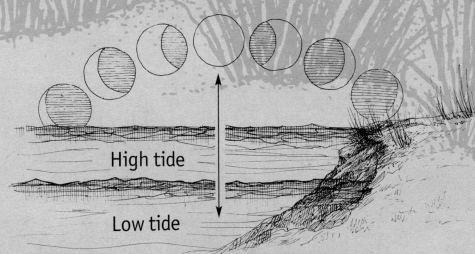
Rockfish

The Chesapeake Bay is really a flooded river valley. Until 10,000 years ago, the Susquehanna River flowed to the ocean where the bay is now. As *glaciers* melted at the end of the last ice age, the ocean level rose and flooded the Susquehanna River Valley.

The bay is a mixture of fresh water from rivers and salt water from the ocean. Like the ocean, the Chesapeake Bay has tides. The ocean's high tide pushes more water into the bay. When the ocean's tide goes out, the water from the bay rushes after it. This is called low tide.

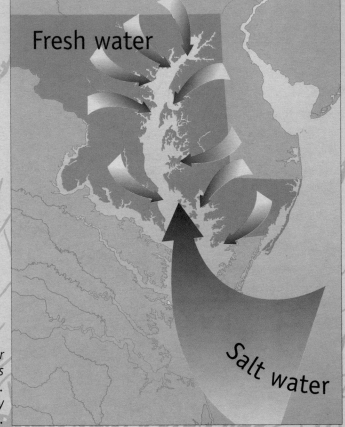
Fresh water

Salt water

▲ Photos of rockfish and blue crab by George Grall, Courtesy of the National Aquarium in Baltimore ▲

High tide

Low tide

Tides are affected by the moon. When the moon is full, the high tide is very high and the low tide is very low. Between the full moons, the high tides are not quite as high and the low tides are not quite as low.

Did you know that there are islands in the Chesapeake Bay? The largest is Kent Island.

Blue crab

Keeping the Bay Clean

We eat shellfish such as oysters, clams, and crabs from the bay. We also eat rockfish, bluefish, and perch from the bay. These fish eat smaller fish such as anchovies and menhaden. Some small fish eat tiny plants that float in the water.

However, we are finding fewer fish and shellfish today. One reason is that people have been catching too much seafood. We have caught so many fish and shellfish that there are not enough left to keep up the population.

The other reason is that the water is often polluted. This destroys the oxygen that fish and shellfish need to breathe. Polluted water can also block the sun's light. Without sun, underwater plants cannot grow. Grasses that grow in shallow parts of the bay are especially important because fish and shellfish often raise their young there.

All of us can do our part to protect the Chesapeake Bay. What can you do?

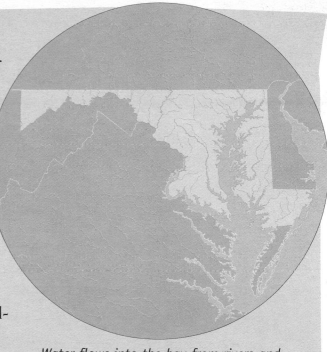

*Water flows into the bay from rivers and streams in many states. These are **tributaries** of the bay. It takes a lot of clean tributaries to make a clean bay.*

There are lots of ways to have fun on the water.

Many people work on the bay. These men are harvesting oysters.

It's a Fact!

The Chesapeake Bay . . .
- is 200 miles long.
- is 4 miles wide near Annapolis.
- is 30 miles wide at its southern end.
- holds 18 trillion gallons of water.

Our Climate

Climate is very important to a place. Look at where Maryland sits on a map or globe. It is in the middle of North America. It is not too close to the equator, where it is warm all year. It is not too close to either the North or South Pole, where it is cold all year. Maryland is in the *Temperate* Zone.

Although the entire state is in the Temperate Zone, the climate does change from region to region. There are several reasons for this:

Distance from large bodies of water. Large bodies of water change temperature more slowly than air does. The water helps keep nearby places cooler in the summer and warmer in the winter. That's why the Eastern Shore has the mildest winters in the state.

Elevation. How high the land is also plays a role in climate. High mountains are colder than lowlands. Maryland's mountains are colder than its beaches. The Appalachian region has the coldest winters in the state and the most snow. Skiing is a popular sport there.

Do you know the difference between climate and weather? Climate is the big picture, year after year. Weather is what we get each day. Each day's weather can be sunny or rainy, warm or cool, windy or calm.

Sometimes in Maryland we have dangerous weather. Hurricanes, ice storms, and *droughts*—when there is not enough rain—cause serious problems. We cannot control the weather, but we can try to be prepared for the problems it may bring.

Highest Point:
● Backbone Mountain, 3,360 feet

Lowest Point: Atlantic Coast, Sea Level

Ten inches of snow provide the same amount of water as one inch of rain.

Precipitation

Precipitation is water in the form of rain, snow, sleet, or hail. Places with a temperate climate usually have enough precipitation to support the needs of their people, animals, and plants. This is true in Maryland. We get about the same amount of water every month of the year. We do not have a rainy season or a dry season the way some parts of the world do.

In the mountains we can have 100 inches of snowfall in a year. On the Eastern Shore there may be only ten inches of snow in a winter, but there is more rain.

Which season is shown here at Swallow Falls State Park?

Photos by Middleton Evans

Places in the Temperate Zone have four seasons: winter, spring, summer, and fall. Which season is shown here along the Potomac River?

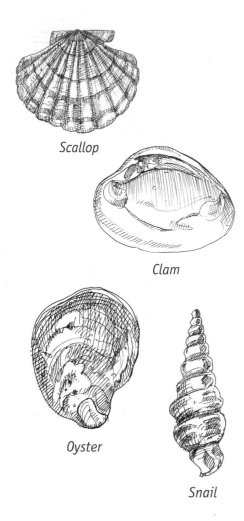

Scallop

Clam

Oyster

Snail

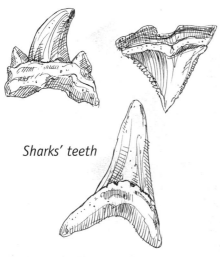

Sharks' teeth

These are some of the most common fossils found in Maryland.

ANIMALS AND PLANTS

We share our home with other species. Many different animals and plants live in Maryland. Some of the animals live in homes or on farms. We take care of our dogs and cats, cows and chickens. We feed them and provide them with shelter. Other animals live in the wild and find their own food and shelter.

Some plants grow on farms or in people's gardens. Farmers grow wheat, corn, and soybeans. In our gardens we grow flowers and vegetables. Many plants grow wild in fields and woods and wetlands across the state.

Ancient Animals

Animals lived in what is now Maryland long before any people lived here. They roamed the land and swam in the water. These animals are now *extinct*. They no longer live anywhere on earth.

How do we know about creatures that lived all those millions of years ago? We don't have photographs or written records from way back then. We have to use clues to figure out what life was like. We have to be detectives. The most important clues are *fossils*, left from thousands or millions of years ago.

Some fossils are the remains of animal bones or teeth. Others are imprints of the remains. These are like footprints. When you walk through wet sand or cement, you leave a footprint.

▲ Photo by Middleton Evans

Horseshoe crabs have swum in the ocean since the time of the dinosaurs. In recent years, people have caught them and chopped them up for fish bait. We should be careful not to kill all these amazing animals that have survived for millions of years.

Sometimes scientists find footprints where dinosaurs walked. A bone or the leaf of a plant can also leave a "footprint." Fossils help us know what life was like millions of years ago.

Millions of years ago, dinosaurs lived all over North America. There were dinosaurs in what is now Maryland.   Have you ever seen a dinosaur? Actually, you have! Their relatives live on as birds. The first birds were flying reptiles. Even though dinosaurs became extinct about 65 million years ago, the birds that fly today share a common *ancestor* with the last of the dinosaurs.

Mammoths, mastodons, saber-toothed tigers, and other ancient animals lived in Maryland millions of years after the dinosaurs disappeared. Their relatives, modern elephants and tigers, still live on earth, but not in Maryland.

Several ancient animals do still live with us. They look much like their ancestors did long ago. Dragonflies, cockroaches, horse-shoe crabs, and sharks have survived for millions of years.

The earliest people hunted mammoths and saber-toothed tigers. These animals are now extinct.

Ancient fish still swim in the Chesapeake Bay. You can see a gar and sturgeon at the National Aquarium in Baltimore. Their thick skin helps them defend themselves.

▼ Photos by George Grall, Courtesy of the National Aquarium in Baltimore

Calvert Cliffs

We can find fossils right here in Maryland. Long ago, when the glaciers melted, the ocean level rose. Part of the East Coast was under the water. Shells and bones of dead animals sank to the bottom and were covered by sand and mud. The level of the ocean changed many times.

What was once the bottom of the sea is now found on the face of the Calvert Cliffs. You can find fossil shells, bones, and even sharks' teeth on the beach. Would you be excited to find five-inch-long teeth from a great white shark and bones from whales and dolphins?

These fossils were found in the cliffs.

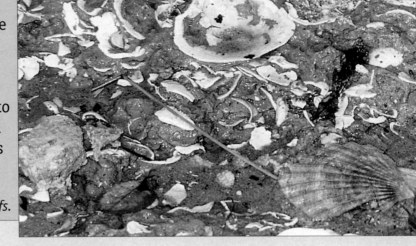

▲ Photo of fossils by Suzanne Chapelle

Calvert Cliffs were once under water.

The Maryland Adventure

Astrodons

Astrodon johnstoni is Maryland's official state dinosaur. Fossils of this dinosaur have been found along "Dinosaur Alley." Our state dinosaur was forty feet tall, sixty feet long, and weighed ten tons. It could run at a speed of eighteen miles an hour.

The *Astrodon* lived in forests. It ate leaves from the tops of tall trees. Sometimes it reached down and ate water lilies. Because *Astrodon johnstoni* did not have the kind of teeth that could grind up all the leaves it ate, it swallowed stones to help crush the food in its stomach.

Dinosaur Alley

Dinosaur tracks, teeth, bones, and shells have been found in "Dinosaur Alley."

This painting of young Astrodons *is part of a dinosaur show at the Maryland Science Center in Baltimore.*

Maryland's Animals Today

When you wake up in the morning, listen to the birds singing outside. Hundreds of different kinds of birds live in Maryland. Some of them stay here all year round. Some spend only the summer or winter here. Others pass through in the fall and spring as they *migrate* from Canada to places farther south.

Water Birds

Ducks, geese, swans, egrets, and herons live near the water. Much of their food comes from the water. Brown pelicans now live along the coast of Maryland during the summer. Seagulls live by the ocean and across much of Maryland.

▲ Photos by Middleton Evans ▶

Tundra swans and Canada geese are seen in many places near water.

Great blue herons live along the coast.

The Maryland Adventure

Raptors

Many birds in Maryland are birds of prey, called raptors. They swoop down and catch small animals or fish in their beaks or claws. Then they take them to a safe place and eat them. Hawks, owls, peregrine falcons, ospreys, and bald eagles are raptors that live in Maryland.

Owls hunt at night. They have excellent eyesight. They can see small animals such as mice from a great distance.

Peregrine falcons used to live on high cliffs. Today some make their homes on tall buildings and bridge towers. These falcons live high up on a building in downtown Baltimore. They eat pigeons and other city birds.

The bald eagle, our national bird, was almost extinct. Today bald eagles nest in Maryland. Many live near the Chesapeake Bay.

Fish, Shellfish, and Marine Mammals

Because Maryland has so much water around it, fish, shellfish, and marine mammals live here. Some fish, such as trout, live in freshwater streams. Others, such as rockfish, bluefish, and flounder, live in salt water. Shellfish—blue crabs, oysters, and clams—live in our bays.

Some fish live in both fresh and salt water. For example, shad and herring are born in fresh water. They swim to the salty bay or ocean and live there for most of their lives. Then they return to the stream where they were born to have their young. These fish have a big problem when a dam blocks their route back upstream.

Marine mammals such as dolphins and whales travel along the Atlantic Coast and sometimes into the Chesapeake Bay. During the summer, if you sit on the beach and watch closely, you may see dolphins swim by. In cold weather, the dolphins migrate south to warmer waters.

Whales usually swim out in deep water. Seals also live in the Atlantic Ocean. Sometimes they come to sit on the beach. Several kinds of sea turtles swim in Maryland's waters.

"I pulled a three-foot fish from the water, and it was flopping all over the place. I jumped up and down, screaming. It was a real shame that there was not one single person to see me and my fish."

—*Michael Batty*

Because we eat fish and shellfish, it is important to keep the water they live in clean.

▲ Photo by Yuri Huta

Dolphins from the Atlantic Ocean sometimes swim into the Chesapeake Bay.

▶ Photos by Middleton Evans

Wild ponies

Black bear

Red fox

White-tailed deer

Opossums

Mammals

Most mammals live on the land. These animals nurse their young. Most of them have fur. Can you name some mammals that live in Maryland? If you named squirrels, chipmunks, rabbits, mice, groundhogs, opossums, beavers, foxes, and raccoons, you are correct. You are also correct if you named larger animals like deer and black bears. These animals live in the woods and fields.

Because so much of our land is now covered with buildings, some animals have learned to live in the city and suburbs. What wild animals live near your home?

Other Animals

As you can see, a lot of different animals live in Maryland. Frogs and toads and snakes and turtles live here. And we haven't even mentioned the insects. Thousands of tiny insects live here. We share our state with many creatures, large and small.

▶ Monarch butterfly photo by Keith Harrison

Monarch bullerflies soar through Maryland in the fall. They are on their way to their winter home in Mexico. Can you imagine how this small butterfly travels such a long distance?

Natural Maryland

Maryland's Plants

Plants are an important part of Maryland's natural environment. Trees, bushes, vegetables, and flowers are all plants. Without plants, people and animals could not survive.

Some plants are found all over the state. Others grow only in places where the climate or the soil suits them best. Some plants like wetlands. Other plants like dry rocky soil. Still others like the mix of clay and sand that is found in much of Maryland's farmland.

Some plants are *native* to Maryland. That means they have always lived here. They live well in our climate. Many of them provide food for our native animals.

Do you like juicy blueberries, blackberries, and strawberries? These plants are native to Maryland. Other common native plants are white pines, American hollies, milkweed, salt marsh cordgrass, black-eyed Susans, and sunflowers.

Battle Creek Swamp is farther north than any other cypress swamp in the country.

Sunflowers and bald cypress trees grow naturally in Maryland.

▲ Photos by Middleton Evans

Photo by Mame Warren

The Wye Oak in Talbot County is the largest white oak tree in the state. It is over 400 years old. The tree has lived through a lot of history. White oaks are native to Maryland. Today you can buy trees grown from Wye Oak acorns.

Natural Maryland

REGIONS

A region is another way to describe where we live. Places that are alike in some way are called regions. A place can be in many regions at the same time. For example, Marylanders live in the eastern region of the United States. Some of us live east of the Chesapeake Bay. That region is called the Eastern Shore. Others live west of the Chesapeake Bay. That is the Western Shore region.

Many Marylanders live in urban regions. These are the areas in or around cities. People on farms live in rural regions. What regions do you live in?

Land Regions

Maryland is divided into three major landform regions. Each region has a different type of land, such as flat fields, rolling hills, or mountains. The three main land regions in Maryland are the Atlantic Coastal Plain, the Piedmont Plateau, and the Appalachian region.

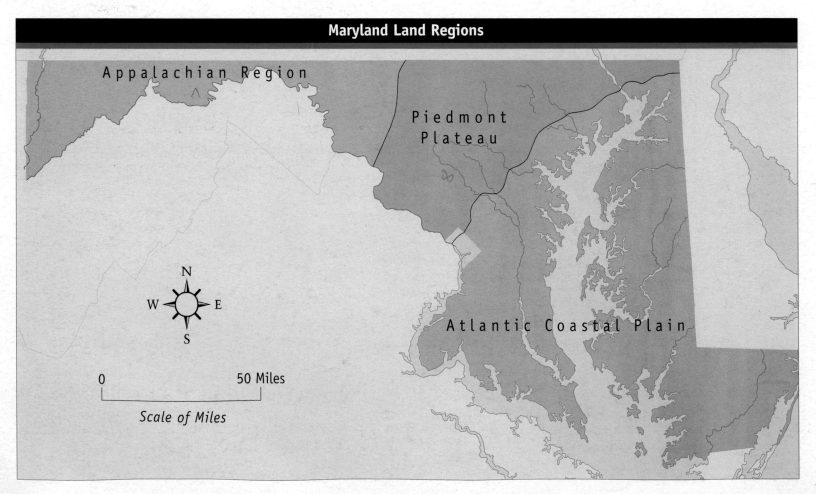

Maryland Land Regions

Appalachian Region

Piedmont Plateau

Atlantic Coastal Plain

0   50 Miles

Scale of Miles

Assateague Island's wide beach and sand dunes are part of the Atlantic Coastal Plain. Behind it, you can see Ocean City with its man-made features. How are these places different from each other?

The Atlantic Coastal Plain

Some of us live on the Atlantic Coastal Plain. Some of us cross it every summer going to the ocean. The Atlantic Coastal Plain begins at the wide flat beaches along the Atlantic Ocean. It stretches west across the Chesapeake Bay until the land becomes hilly. Our state capital, Annapolis, is in the Atlantic Coastal Plain region.

A long time ago, when only a few people lived in this region, the land was mostly wetlands and forests. When more and more people came and settled here, they filled in the wetlands to build towns along the water's edge. Farmers cut down forests to make space for their fields.

The soil on the Atlantic Coastal Plain is light and good for farming. Crops such as corn, soybeans, melons, tomatoes, and squash grow well there.

Towns and farms are very important to us. We live in towns and eat food grown on the farms. Wetlands and forests are also important. They are home to many animals and plants. They help

Fertile *fields cover much of the Atlantic Coastal Plain.*

clean the water that flows through them. They help protect us by absorbing water when there is a flood. Forests help clean the air that we breathe. We must take care of our wetlands and forests just as we take care of our towns and farms.

Natural Maryland

The Piedmont Plateau

Many of us live in the Piedmont Plateau region. This part of Maryland has the *densest* population. That means it has the most people for its size. Many towns and cities have been built there.

In the Piedmont Plateau region, the land is higher than the Atlantic Coastal Plain. The soil is rockier, too, but it is very fertile. Wheat grows very well there. So do corn, vegetables, and many fruits.

Gently rolling hills and valleys cross the Piedmont Plateau. Streams flow down the hills into Maryland's big rivers.

Maryland Fall Line

Baltimore

Ellicott City

Washington, D.C.

The Piedmont Plateau begins at the *fall line* on the east. The fall line is an important natural feature. When a stream or river flows downhill over rocks, there is a waterfall or rapids. If you placed an "x" on the first falls of each river, then connected the "x"s, you would draw the fall line.

Waterfalls and rapids are important to people. Falling water can make power for electricity to run machines. There is flat, calm water just below the falls. That is a good place for boats.

Long ago, the Piedmont Plateau was mostly forest. Most of the forests were cut down as people built homes, farms, mills, factories, offices, and stores.

The hilly northern and western parts of Baltimore are in the Piedmont Plateau. Baltimore is in a very good location. Ships can cross the Atlantic Ocean, sail up the Chesapeake Bay, and go right into the harbor.

Farmers sell their fruits and vegetables at markets like this one. What are your favorite fruits and vegetables?

The Appalachian Region

The Appalachian region is in western Maryland. It has the highest elevation of any part of the state. Most of the land is at least 500 feet above sea level.

The region is heavily forested with oak, hickory, and hemlock trees. Many small streams flow downhill into larger streams and rivers.

Coal is found in the Appalachian region. A newer source of power—natural gas—is also found there. It burns more cleanly than coal and is widely used today.

The Appalachian region is made up of four smaller regions. If you drive westward across the state, the first mountains you will see are the **Blue Ridge Mountains**. The mountains are covered with beautiful green forests. American presidents come here to a place called Camp David. At Camp David, presidents and their guests can walk through the woods and have long talks away from the busy city of Washington, D.C.

West of the Blue Ridge Mountains is the **Great Valley**. This wide valley was a good place for early settlers moving west to build new homes. The fertile soil is good for growing wheat and apples.

Further west are higher mountains. These are the **Valleys and Ridges**. The **Allegheny Plateau** lies west of Cumberland. Backbone Mountain is there. It rises to 3,360 feet above sea level.

Maryland's highest mountains are in the Appalachian region.

At Deep Creek Lake you can go water skiing, boating, fishing, or swimming.

MOVEMENT

When people travel from place to place, they take their ideas with them. They share information with others. Early people traveled great distances. They traded ideas and tools with other groups. This made them better hunters, fishermen, craftsmen, and farmers.

Today, people and goods from countries all over the world move in and out of Maryland. Some people stay for a short time to do business or take a vacation. Others come here to live. Movement of goods and information links Maryland with all parts of the world.

RELATIONSHIPS

People, animals, and plants all live on the land together. Geographers study the relationship between the land, people, animals, and plants.

Ecosystems

An *ecosystem* is a community. It includes the animals, plants, soil, water, and air that interact with each other. Every living creature is part of an ecosystem. Human beings, animals, and plants get everything they need to live from their ecosystem. They also put things back into the ecosystem.

An ecosystem contains many kinds of life. Each part does its own special job. Some animals, called *predators*, eat smaller animals. Some animals eat only plants. Plants depend on soil that has been made richer by dead animals and plants. They need this rich soil to grow.

As we study the history of Maryland, you will see that the natural environment is important to all of us. You will learn some of the ways that people have changed the environment and the results these changes have had.

Trash Can Hurt Animals

Do you know that a balloon that blows away or an old plastic bag can be a real danger to dolphins, whales, and turtles? They might eat the plastic, mistaking it for a yummy jellyfish. The animal may die because the plastic sticks in its stomach.

- What do you think we should do with our trash?
- Do you think releasing balloons into the air is a good or bad idea? Why?

Drawings by Gary Rasmussen

All parts of nature work together in an ecosystem.

Threatened and Endangered Species

An **endangered** species is an animal or plant that is in danger of becoming extinct. That means that this kind of animal or plant might die soon. "Extinct" is forever.

All over the world there are animals, birds, fish, reptiles, insects, and plants that are in danger of disappearing forever. A species that is close to becoming endangered is called "threatened." Examples in Maryland include peregrine falcons and shortnose sturgeons.

One reason that some animals and plants are in danger of dying off is that their habitats or homes are disappearing. As we cut down forests and fill in wetlands, these species no longer have a home. Our country and our state have made laws to help protect threatened and endangered plants and animals.

Eastern cougar

Eastern tiger salamander

Bog turtle

Bald eagle

Snow trillium

Indiana bat

Peregrine falcon

Delmarva fox squirrel

Small white lady's slipper

Indian paintbrush

Shortnose sturgeon

Sperm whale

Piping plover

Sources: U.S. Fish and Wildlife Service and Maryland Department of Natural Resources

▲ Drawings by Gary Rasmussen

The Maryland Adventure

Water Pollution

The ocean begins right on your street. That's right! Rain water flows down into the storm sewer. It washes trash along with it. The storm water flows into the nearest stream. The stream water flows into a big river, which flows into the Chesapeake Bay. The Chesapeake Bay flows into the ocean. Stream or sewer water may also end up in a lake where your drinking water comes from. How can we help keep our water clean?

When people leave trash around, it enters the storm sewers.

The sewers lead to streams and rivers.

You can help keep our water clean. Always put your trash where it belongs—in a trash can!

This is what can happen to beaches and riverbanks if trash is left lying around.

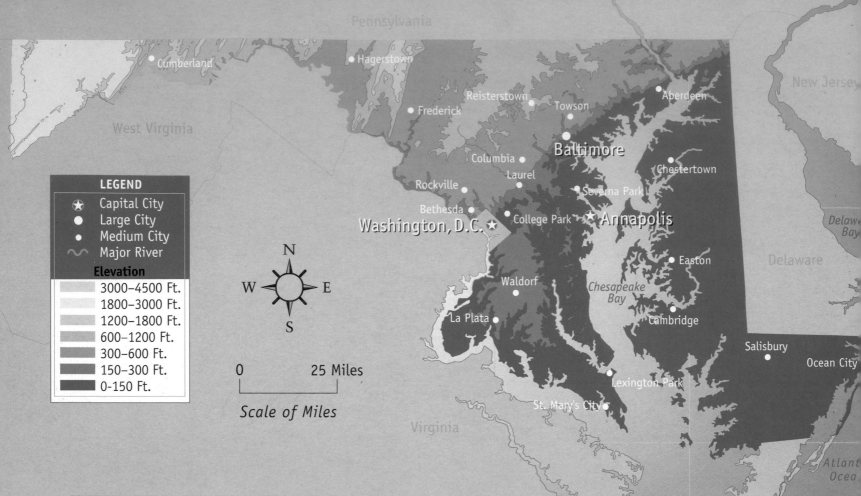

Activity

Reading a Map

Maps help us understand where we are. They help us get where we want to go. It is important to know how to read a map. Most maps have the following features:

Compass Maps show the directions north, south, east, and west. You'll find these directions on a symbol called a compass. Find the compass on the map.

Most maps have north at the top. A map is much easier to read if you put it so that you and the map are facing north. Then west will be on your left and east will be on your right. Where will south be?

Legend or Key Map makers use symbols so they don't have to write words all over the map. The symbols stand for things such as cities, rivers, airports, and campgrounds. Whenever there are symbols, there is a key or legend that explains what the symbols mean. What do the symbols on this map stand for?

Scale of Miles To show us how far apart things are, map makers use a scale of miles. This helps us measure the distance between places. One inch on a map might stand for 100 miles on real land. Or one inch might mean 1,000 miles or even more.

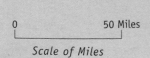

Look at the map. How many miles are equal to one inch on the scale of miles? How many miles are between Baltimore and Washington, D.C.? Between Rockville and Cumberland? Which is the shorter distance?

Geography Bowl

Divide your class into four teams. Ask each team three questions. All members of the team must work together to get the answers. Then a spokesperson for the team gives the answers.

1. Name a raptor that lives in Maryland and eats fish.
2. Name an insect that flies south to spend the winter.
3. Name a small, gray, furry endangered animal.

1. Which land region has beaches and flat farmland?
2. Which land region has the highest mountains?
3. Which land region has the densest population?

1. The Chesapeake Bay used to be the valley of which river?
2. Name Maryland's state dinosaur.
3. Where can you go to look for fossils of sharks' teeth?

1. What is a continent?
2. What is a peninsula?
3. What is a fall line?

Questions for Review

1. What is geography?
2. List some natural features of Maryland. List some human features of Maryland.
3. What are some reasons why the Chesapeake Bay is important?
4. What are two things that affect our climate?
5. List two extinct animals that lived in Maryland long ago.
6. List some wild animals that live in Maryland. Which ones have you seen?
7. What is the word that describes plants that have always lived here?
8. List Maryland's three major land regions. Which land region do you live in?
9. Why is it important for us to protect natural ecosystems?
10. What are some ways we can protect our environment?

THE TIME
12,000 B.C.–A.D. 1700

PEOPLE TO KNOW
Paleo-Indians
Archaic Indians
Woodland Indians
Nanticokes
Piscataways
Shawnees
Iroquois
Susquehannocks
Lumbees

PLACES TO LOCATE
Asia
Chesapeake Bay
Europe
Susquehanna River
Pennsylvania
Potomac River
Delaware
North Carolina

The First People

timeline of events

12,000 B.C.

8,000 B.C.
Glaciers begin to melt.
The Chesapeake Bay is formed.
Forests take the place of grasslands.

8,000 B.C.

4,000 B.C.

12,000 B.C.
Paleo-Indians live all
over America. They are
the first people in the
land we call Maryland.

8,000 B.C.–1,000 B.C.
Archaic Indians live in bands of
twenty-five to fifty people.

This picture of a Woodland Indian village was drawn by an Englishman named John White in 1585.

chapter 2

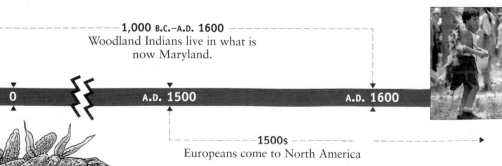

1,000 B.C.–A.D. 1600
Woodland Indians live in what is now Maryland.

| 0 | A.D. 1500 | A.D. 1600 | A.D. 1700 |

1500s
Europeans come to North America

A.D. 1700
Only a few Indians still live in Maryland.

EARLY PEOPLE LIVED HERE

SCIENTISTS BELIEVE that the first people in North America came from Asia. They arrived on foot many thousands of years ago. People can no longer walk from Asia to America. When the glaciers melted at the end of the last ice age, water covered the narrow bridge of land that had connected Asia and North America.

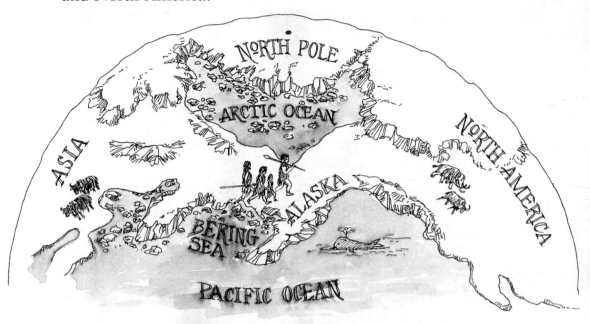

Long ago, people walked from Asia to North America. Over time, they spread out all over North and South America.

Paleo-Indians

We call the first people who lived here the Paleo-Indians. "Paleo" means ancient, or very old.

Paleo-Indians reached the land we call Maryland about 14,000 years ago. At that time, the climate was much colder than it is today. Huge glaciers were not far away. The Chesapeake Bay was still a river valley.

When the climate was cold, grasslands spread across the land. Giant animals such as woolly mammoths and saber-toothed tigers lived here. The Paleo-Indians hunted these animals for food. They also hunted white-tailed deer. They caught fish from the rivers. They gathered berries, nuts, leaves, and roots from plants. People who hunt and gather their food are called *hunter-gatherers*.

The people could not have lived without plants. They learned how to use the roots, stems, flowers, and leaves.

▲ Drawings by Gary Rasmussen ▶

The Maryland Adventure

Paleo-Indians made tools from stone. They used very hard stones to chip other stones until they had a sharp edge. They made knives and points for their spears. They made scrapers to scrape animal hides that they wore as clothing.

Archaic Indians

As time passed, the climate in North America began to change. The temperature grew warmer. The glaciers began to melt. The water formed new rivers and lakes. More trees grew.

Many of the giant mammals became extinct in North America. Some people believe that the animals could not live in the warmer climate. Others believe that people hunted the animals until they were gone. Deer became a major source of food. As the Chesapeake Bay grew larger, people began to harvest shellfish such as oysters and clams.

The people still gathered plants for food. They knew which ones were good to eat and which were not. They figured out how to grind seeds and nuts into flour to make a kind of bread.

Archaic Indians lived in small groups. Like the Paleo-Indians, they traveled to different places to get the food that was available at different times of the year. They hunted with spears, built fish traps and nets, and made canoes. They carved bowls from a soft rock called soapstone.

The people made a tool called an **atlatl**, or spear thrower. It let a hunter throw his spear the length of a football field. Do you think it would be a good idea to keep a distance between the hunter and a large animal? Why?

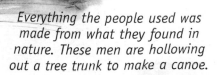

Everything the people used was made from what they found in nature. These men are hollowing out a tree trunk to make a canoe.

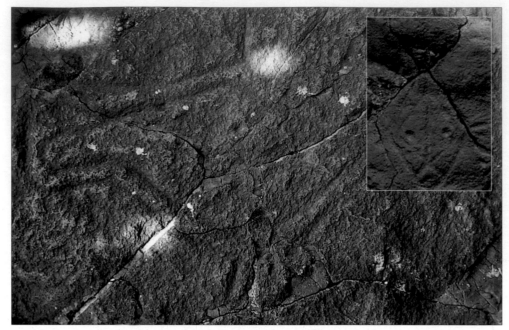

*These **petroglyphs** were left on rocks in what is now Maryland. What do you think they mean?*

The people chipped sharp edges around hard rock to make scrapers and spear points. The scrapers took the fur off animal skins.

Linking the past to the present

About 12,000 American Indians lived in Maryland when the European colonists arrived. Can you find out how many people live in Maryland today?

How Do We Know?

How do we know so much about people who lived so long ago? They did not leave any photos or written records. But they did leave behind clues about how they lived.

The people left **artifacts** that tell us a lot of information. Artifacts are spear points, stone tools, bowls—anything the people made and left behind. Ancient people also left drawings on rocks and in caves. **Archaeologists** study these clues to learn about the men, women, and children who lived long ago.

WOODLAND INDIANS

The people who lived in what is now the eastern United States about 3,000 years ago are called Woodland Indians.

The Woodland Indians' most important new idea was agriculture, or farming. The people still hunted and gathered food, but they began to grow food, too. Because they grew crops, people could settle down in one place. They no longer had to travel all over to find enough to eat. However, they did still travel to find wild animals to hunt. Perhaps because there was more food, the population grew.

Woodland Indians were living here when ships from Europe arrived. Europeans claimed to have discovered a new land. The Indians knew this land was here all along. It was their home.

Children had the important job of guarding the crops.

What do you think?

Why do you think the Indians who lived in our region are called Woodland Indians?

Villages, Tribes, and Nations

Most Woodland Indians lived in a village. Like our towns and cities, each village had a name. Each village was part of a larger group. In English, we often call that group a tribe. Members of a tribe shared a *lifestyle* and a common language. Often a number of tribes spoke languages that were very similar to each other. Sometimes these tribes joined together in larger groups called nations.

Woodland Tribes in Maryland

In the land we call Maryland, there were several Woodland tribes. The largest group of Woodland Indians on the Eastern Shore was the Nanticoke tribe. Smaller tribes became their *allies*. They agreed to protect each other and work together for a common goal.

The largest tribe on the Western Shore was the Piscataway. They also had smaller tribes as allies. At certain times in history, Shawnee Indians also lived in western Maryland. All these people spoke languages in the Algonquin [al GON kin] family.

Nation
▼
▼
▼
Tribe
▼
▼
▼
Village

Farther north were the Susquehannocks. Their language was different from the other tribes. It was part of the Iroquois language family. However, the Susquehannocks were not part of the large Iroquois nation.

Susquehannocks built villages along the Susquehanna River in what is now Pennsylvania. They also had some villages along the Potomac River. When they hunted, they traveled into territory that the Nanticokes and the Piscataways considered theirs. Sometimes there were wars. The Susquehannocks were known as fierce fighters.

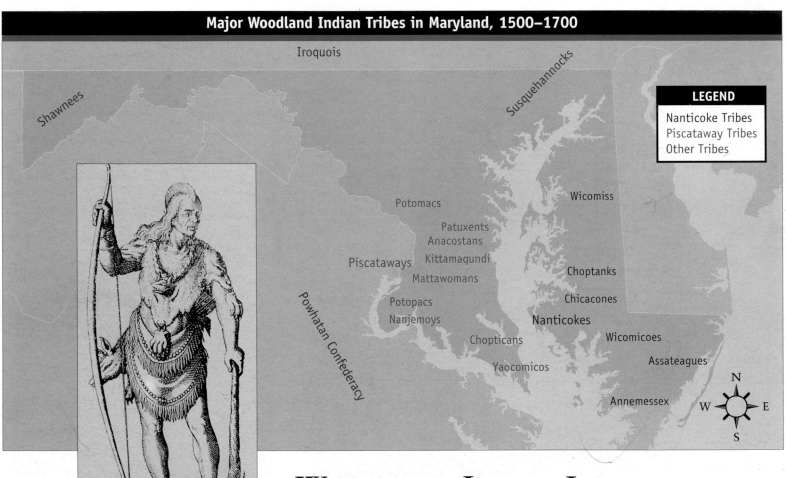

Major Woodland Indian Tribes in Maryland, 1500–1700

Iroquois

Shawnees

Susquehannocks

LEGEND
Nanticoke Tribes
Piscataway Tribes
Other Tribes

Potomacs

Wicomiss

Patuxents
Anacostans
Piscataways Kittamaqundi

Choptanks

Mattawomans

Powhatan Confederacy

Potopacs

Chicacones

Nanjemoys

Nanticokes

Chopticans

Wicomicoes

Yaocomicos

Assateagues

Annemessex

N
W   E
S

This Susquehannock man is carrying his bow, his club, and an animal he killed during the hunt.

WOODLAND INDIAN LIFE

Woodland Indians had the same needs that we all share. To survive, they needed shelter, food, and water. They had to have clothing to keep warm. They needed tools to help them do their work. Today we can go to the store to buy things. The Indian people learned to use the natural materials they could find nearby.

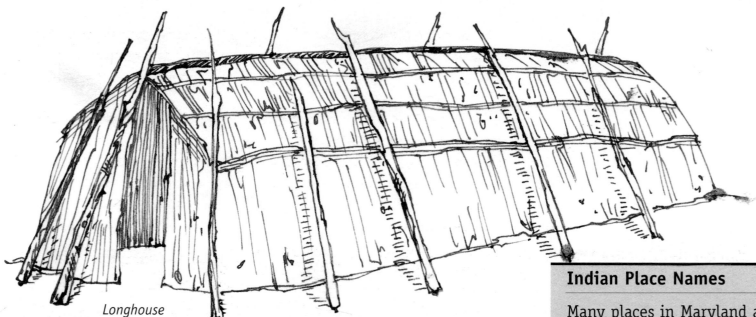

Longhouse

Building a Home

The Woodland Indians lived in wigwams or longhouses. They made their homes of wood, bark, and grasses. The chief or village leader usually had the largest home.

Inside the wigwam, there was not much furniture. People built platforms around the walls. They covered these with grass mats or animal skins. They sat and slept on the platforms.

The people built a fire in the center of the wigwam. They used it for heat and cooking. They left an opening in the roof so the smoke could get out. When it rained or snowed, they covered the hole. The homes were hot and smoky. In good weather, people cooked and ate outdoors.

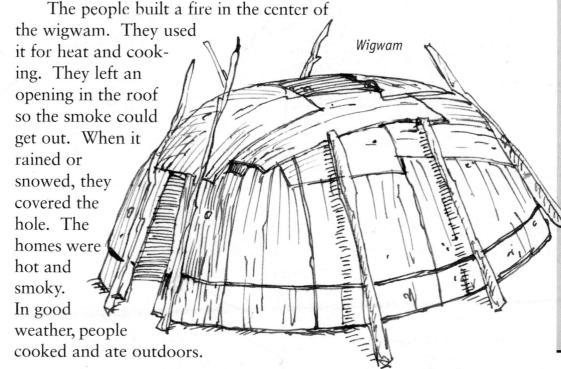

Wigwam

Indian Place Names

Many places in Maryland are still called by their Indian names. These names often describe the place. Here are a few examples:

Wicomico = pleasant dwelling place

Nanticoke = tidal river or waves

Chesapeake = great shell-fish bay

Potomac = where the goods are brought in

Kittamaqundi = place of the Great Old Beaver (The Piscataway ruler was called the Great Old Beaver.)

Susquehanna = smooth flowing stream

Catoctin = speckled mountain

Lonaconing = where there is a beautiful summit

Youghiogheny = it flows with a muddy stream

Drawings by Gary Rasmussen ▶

A Step-by-Step Wigwam

 1 To build a wigwam, the people cut down straight young trees called **saplings**. They trimmed off the branches. Then they dug holes in the ground. They put saplings in the holes. This held the saplings in place.

2 They bent the saplings over, then lashed them together with cord, vines, or animal skins. This made a frame for the wigwam.

▲ Photos by Suzanne Chapelle, Courtesy of the Irvine Natural Science Center

3 Finally, they covered the frame with bark or mats made of grasses and reeds. They left a door and a hole in the top so the smoke from the fire could escape.

Villages

Most Woodland Indians lived in small villages. They built as few as ten or as many as thirty houses. They made their villages near a river or stream. They built on high land, so floods would not wash away their homes.

Usually the homes were built around an open plaza. Sometimes they made a **palisade**, or high fence, around their village for protection. They planted fields near the village. During hunting season everyone moved into **temporary** homes in the forest where the animals lived.

A few bison lived on Maryland's small prairie.

Rivers and Streams

Why did the people build villages near a river or stream? Freshwater rivers and streams gave the people plenty of water to drink. People bathed there, too. They could catch fish to eat. Birds and animals came to the water to drink, so hunting was good there. The people also traveled in canoes on the rivers. It was faster than walking on the land. You can see that there were lots of reasons to build a village near water.

Many American Indians lived near the Chesapeake Bay. They could not drink the salty water, but they found lots of good things to eat there.

*Woodland Indians had several ways of catching fish. They made hooks out of animal bones and put bait on them. They used spears. They also built **weirs** to trap the fish. Weirs have only a small opening. Fish swim in and then cannot find their way out.*

What's for Dinner?

Woodland Indians ate many different kinds of foods. The men and older boys of the village hunted animals such as deer, rabbits, and squirrels. They also brought home birds such as pigeons and wild turkeys. They caught fish. In salt water, they gathered oysters, crabs, and clams.

Near modern Hagerstown there was a small grassy prairie. This was the only part of Maryland where bison lived and could be hunted.

Woodland Indians gathered wild berries. It must have been a special treat to find the sweet berries that were ripe only a few weeks during the spring and summer. People ate roots and leaves. Women and children gathered acorns and chestnuts that grew on oak and chestnut trees. Have you ever picked berries or gathered nuts?

*After the people ate shellfish, they made piles of the empty shells. We call them **middens**. This oyster shell midden is at the Eastern Neck National Wildlife Refuge on the Chesapeake Bay.*

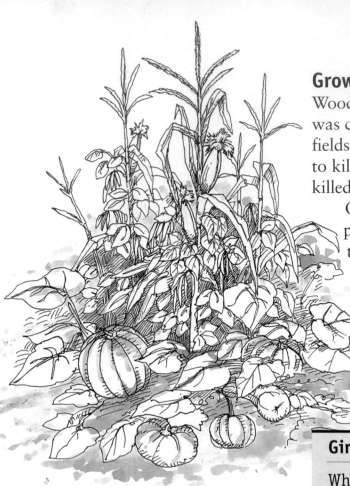

Growing Crops

Woodland Indians began growing food. Since almost all the land was covered with forests, the first job was to clear land for their fields. Crops need sunshine to grow. Sometimes men started fires to kill trees in the area where they wanted to plant. They also killed trees by *girdling* them.

Once the field was clear, the women planted crops. They planted a small hill of corn. When the corn started to grow, they planted beans or peas that would climb the cornstalk. Beans gave nitrogen to the soil. It helped the corn grow. Indians often put small fish in the holes where they planted the corn. It *fertilized* the soil.

Around the hills of corn, women planted squash, pumpkins, and *gourds*. These vines covered the ground between the hills of corn. They helped to keep weeds from growing there.

The "three sisters"—corn, beans and squash—were planted together. The plants helped each other grow. Some farmers and gardeners still plant this way today.

Girdling a Tree

When you girdle a tree, you cut through the bark and the layer of the tree beneath the bark. That second layer is where nourishment flows from the roots up through the tree. If it is destroyed, the tree will die.

Woodland Indians could clear a field without big chainsaws. They just had to cut into the second layer of the tree.

▲ Drawings by Gary Rasmussen

The Maryland Adventure

Children helped grow food for their village. They helped plant the seeds. Later they helped harvest the corn, beans, and squash. Children also helped protect the crops. They sat on a platform in the fields and worked as living scarecrows. If birds or animals came to eat, they waved their arms and yelled loudly until the birds or animals went away.

American Indians grew tobacco. They smoked it in pipes during special ceremonies. Because people rarely smoked it, tobacco did not cause the health problems that it does today.

The people also grew sunflowers. The seeds provided good protein and the roots made a good vegetable.

This boy is grinding corn the same way the Woodland Indians did. They put corn into a hollowed-out log. Using a pole, they ground the kernels into flour. They mixed the flour with water and cooked it on hot rocks to make a kind of bread.

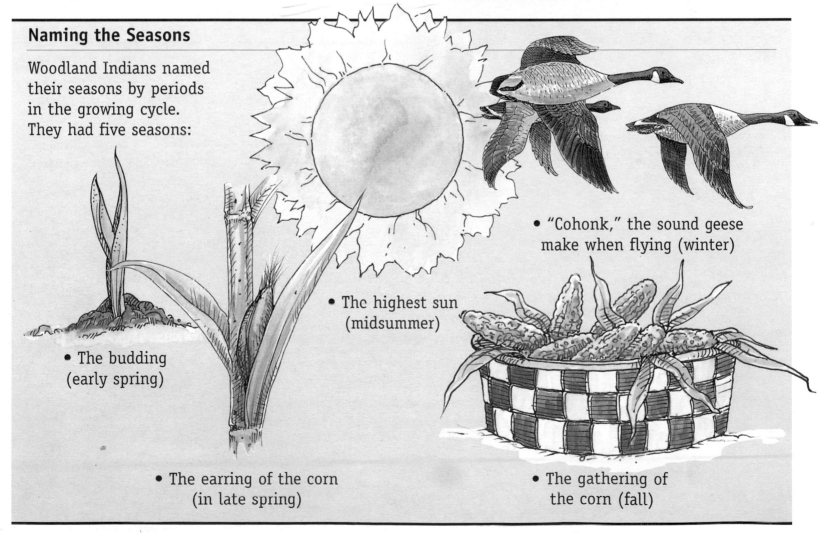

Naming the Seasons

Woodland Indians named their seasons by periods in the growing cycle. They had five seasons:

- The budding (early spring)

- The earring of the corn (in late spring)

- The highest sun (midsummer)

- "Cohonk," the sound geese make when flying (winter)

- The gathering of the corn (fall)

MAKING THINGS FROM NATURE

Today, we buy clothes, furniture, tools, and toys at a store. Because of this, we sometimes forget where things really come from. Everything has to begin with something natural. Wooden toys begin as trees. So does paper. Much of our clothing begins as a plant such as cotton. The Native Americans knew where all the things they used came from because they made clothes and tools themselves.

Making Clothes

Native Americans used every part of the animals they hunted. After eating the meat from a deer, they used the skin for clothing. In the winter, people wore deerskin or bearskin with the fur towards their skin. They made warm leggings and long cloaks.

For summer clothes, women tanned the deerskins. They scraped off the fur. Then they wet and stretched the skins so they would be smooth and light.

During the hot summer, both men and women wore a kind of apron that they tied around their waists. Young children wore very little when the weather was warm.

Indian shoes are called moccasins. These too were made from animal skins.

Like so much in Indian life, making clothes took cooperation. The men and boys hunted. The women and girls sewed the clothing. Men made needles out of animal bones or antlers. Animal *sinews*, or tendons, were used as thread.

Some people today wear make-up and jewelry. Native Americans used face paint for special occasions. Both men and women used natural dyes from plants to tattoo their bodies. In the summer, they rubbed animal grease on their skin to keep away insects.

The people made jewelry, too. They hung stones, shells, animal teeth, and claws around their necks. They used animal teeth and claws as ornaments for their ears. Sometimes they put a few feathers in their hair.

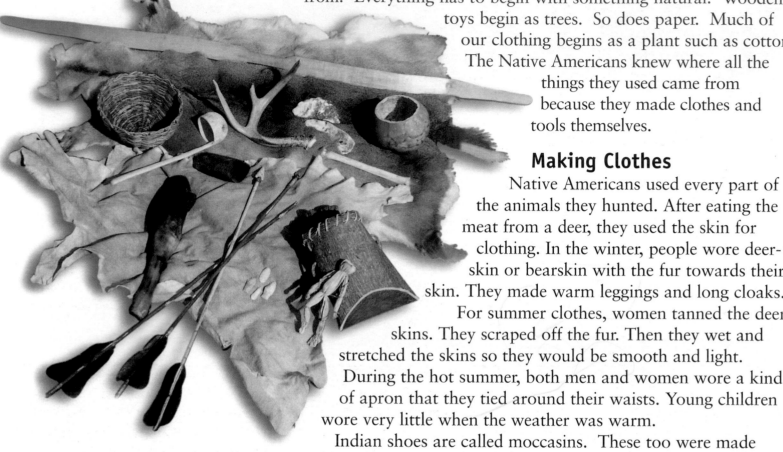

These are modern copies of many things that Native Americans in Maryland made. How do you think each of these things was used?

Making Tools

The people made sewing needles from animal bones. They carved very hard stones to make knives and sharp points for arrows and spears. They stretched animal skins across the top of bowls to make drums. They used antlers to plow the gardens.

Men carved wood into many useful items. They carved ladles to serve soups and stews. They made bows from ash, hickory, and locust trees. They made axes by attaching stones to strong wooden handles.

Women grew gourds in the fields. They saved them until they were dry and hard. Then they used them in a number of ways. Gourds with dried seeds inside were musical instruments. You could shake them like a rattle. A dried gourd served as a bowl or a bottle.

Women gathered grasses, reeds, and bark to make baskets. They made large and small clay pots for cooking and for storing food.

Woodland Indians even made their own boats. Usually they traveled in dugout canoes. For trips on inland waterways, they sometimes made canoes from bark.

If you had to make your own clothes today, what materials would you use?

Making a Dugout Canoe

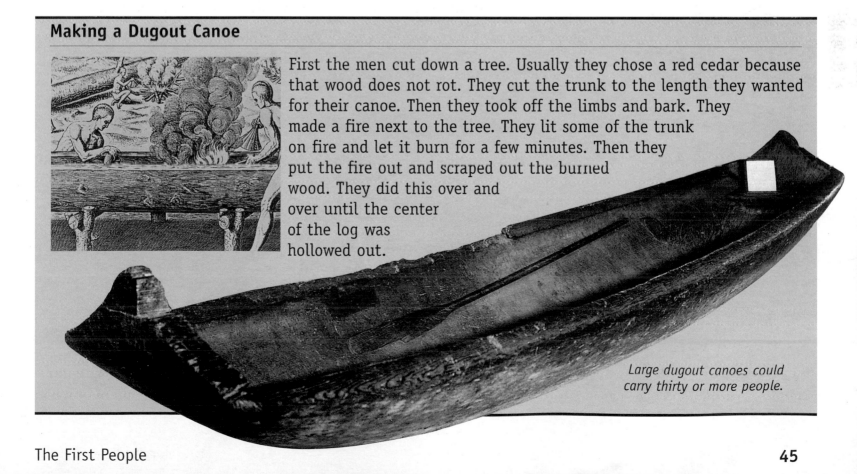

First the men cut down a tree. Usually they chose a red cedar because that wood does not rot. They cut the trunk to the length they wanted for their canoe. Then they took off the limbs and bark. They made a fire next to the tree. They lit some of the trunk on fire and let it burn for a few minutes. Then they put the fire out and scraped out the burned wood. They did this over and over until the center of the log was hollowed out.

Large dugout canoes could carry thirty or more people.

PARTNERS IN VILLAGE LIFE

You can see that children, women, and men all contributed to the life of the village. Everyone shared the work.

Men were responsible for hunting, fishing, clearing fields, and fighting when they needed to. They taught these skills to the boys.

Women were responsible for growing, gathering, and cooking food, sewing clothing, and making pottery. They taught these skills to the girls.

Children had special jobs such as gathering firewood and protecting the fields. They also helped gather food.

Traveling and Trading

People often traveled a long way to trade with their neighbors. The Shawnees had copper jewelry and knives. The Piscataways and Nanticokes had shells. Clam and oyster shells were made into *wampum*. Many Indians used wampum as we use money. Shawnees were eager to trade their copper goods for wampum.

A lot of the traveling was done in canoes along the rivers and up and down the Chesapeake Bay. Sometimes people walked along trails that cut through the forest. Some of the early foot-paths followed animal paths. Some paths later became colonial roads. Many roads today still follow the routes of old Indian trails.

Wampum

There were two kinds of wampum. Peake was the more valuable. It was made of pieces of white or purple shells that were made into beads and strung together. The other kind, roanoke, had unpolished pieces of shell strung on a strip of animal hide. Wampum beads were a sign that a person was being sincere. They were presented during a ceremony to show that the agreement being made was honest.

Waging War

Different tribes could not always agree. Sometimes two or more tribes wanted to use the same land. Sometimes they went to war.

Indians lost family members they loved. Some people were captured and taken prisoner. They were often made slaves by the winning side. Sometimes a prisoner was given to a family that had lost a member during the fighting. The prisoner had to do the dead person's work.

Governing the Tribe

Because there were lots of different Indian tribes, there were lots of different kinds of governments. Most tribes had a peace *council* and a war council. The rulers had many different titles.

The Nanticokes and Piscataways called their leader a *werowance*. Sometimes a woman served as the *werowance*. A *tayac* was the leader of several tribes.

In all tribes, women had some rights and powers. They were often included in making decisions. The village councils discussed things until they could agree on what was best. Chiefs had to talk to priests, warriors, and the tribal councils before they could make important decisions or wage war.

A Spiritual People

Like all people, Native Americans had a set of beliefs about how life began and what happens to us after we die. There were rules about how people should treat each other and the natural world around them.

The people believed that there was a god who had created all life and was the giver of all good things. In the language of some of the tribes, this god was called *Manito*. Shawnees called the creator "Our Grandmother."

Because the creator god had made everything, all living things were sacred and worthy of respect. The first food of the harvest and the first catch of the hunt were always given to the creator in a ceremony of thanksgiving.

The people also believed in an evil spirit, whom some called *Okee*. They gave gifts to *Okee* in hope of escaping troubles.

Curing illness was a kind of religious ceremony. Priests gave herbs to sick people to make them better. They knew which herbs were helpful in curing which illnesses.

Indian Games and Toys

Indian children played games that were fun. The games also taught skills that boys and girls would need when they grew up. They helped the eyes and hands work together. This was an important skill for successful hunting.

Children ran races. Some played lacrosse.

Indian people believed in an afterlife. They believed that the dead would go to a place where good behavior in life would be rewarded or bad behavior would be punished.

PRESERVING A WAY OF LIFE

In the 1600s, many new people began to settle in the land that had been the home of the Nanticokes, Piscataways, Susquehannocks, and Shawnees. Almost right away, everything changed for Native Americans. We will read about how their lives changed in the next chapter.

Native Americans live in Maryland today. Several Piscataway groups live in southern Maryland. They plan events and share their culture with all people. A Nanticoke group lives in Delaware. In recent years, Lumbee Indians from North Carolina have moved to Baltimore City to work. They too want to preserve their culture and share it with other Marylanders. Many people across the state have Indian ancestors. Do you?

What animal materials do you think this boy's costume is made of?

*Modern Piscataways hold **powwows** to preserve their culture. They wear traditional clothing and perform special dances.*

The Maryland Adventure

Family Roles

Men, women, and children were partners in Woodland Indian villages.

1. Name three jobs that men did.
2. Name three jobs that women did.
3. Name three jobs that children did.

Draw pictures that show a man, a woman, a boy, and a girl working at jobs in the village. You may draw four separate pictures, or you may combine several people in one picture. Under each picture, write what the people are doing.

Questions for Review

1. What are the earliest people called?

2. Things made and left behind by people long ago are called _____.

3. Men and women who study these ancient clues are called _____.

4. What was the largest group of Indians living on the Eastern Shore?

5. What was the largest group of Indians living on the Western Shore?

6. Name two kinds of Indian homes and what they were made of.

7. Why were rivers important to the Indian people?

8. What three crops did Woodland Indians often plant together?

9. List five things Indian people made from what they found in nature.

10. What was wampum made from? How was it used?

Geography Tie-In

Study the map on page 38. Then look back at the map on page 22. Use the maps to answer the questions.

1. In what land region of Maryland did most Indians live (around 1600)?

2. Where else in Maryland did people live then?

3. Why do you think they chose these places?

4. On a large wall map of Maryland, find places that have Indian names today.

chapter 3

THE TIME
1590–1750

PEOPLE TO KNOW
Christopher Columbus
Captain John Smith
King Charles I
George Calvert
Cecilius Calvert
Leonard Calvert
Queen Henrietta Marie
Margaret Brent
Jonas Green
Anne Catherine Green
Charles Carroll
Daniel Carroll
Daniel Dulany
Jonathan Hager
Thomas Cresap

PLACES TO LOCATE
Europe
Africa
India
the Americas
Virginia
Chesapeake Bay
St. Clement's Island
St. Mary's City
Annapolis
Oxford
Chestertown
Joppa
Port Tobacco
Baltimore
West Indies
Frederick
Hagerstown
Pennsylvania

Colonial Maryland

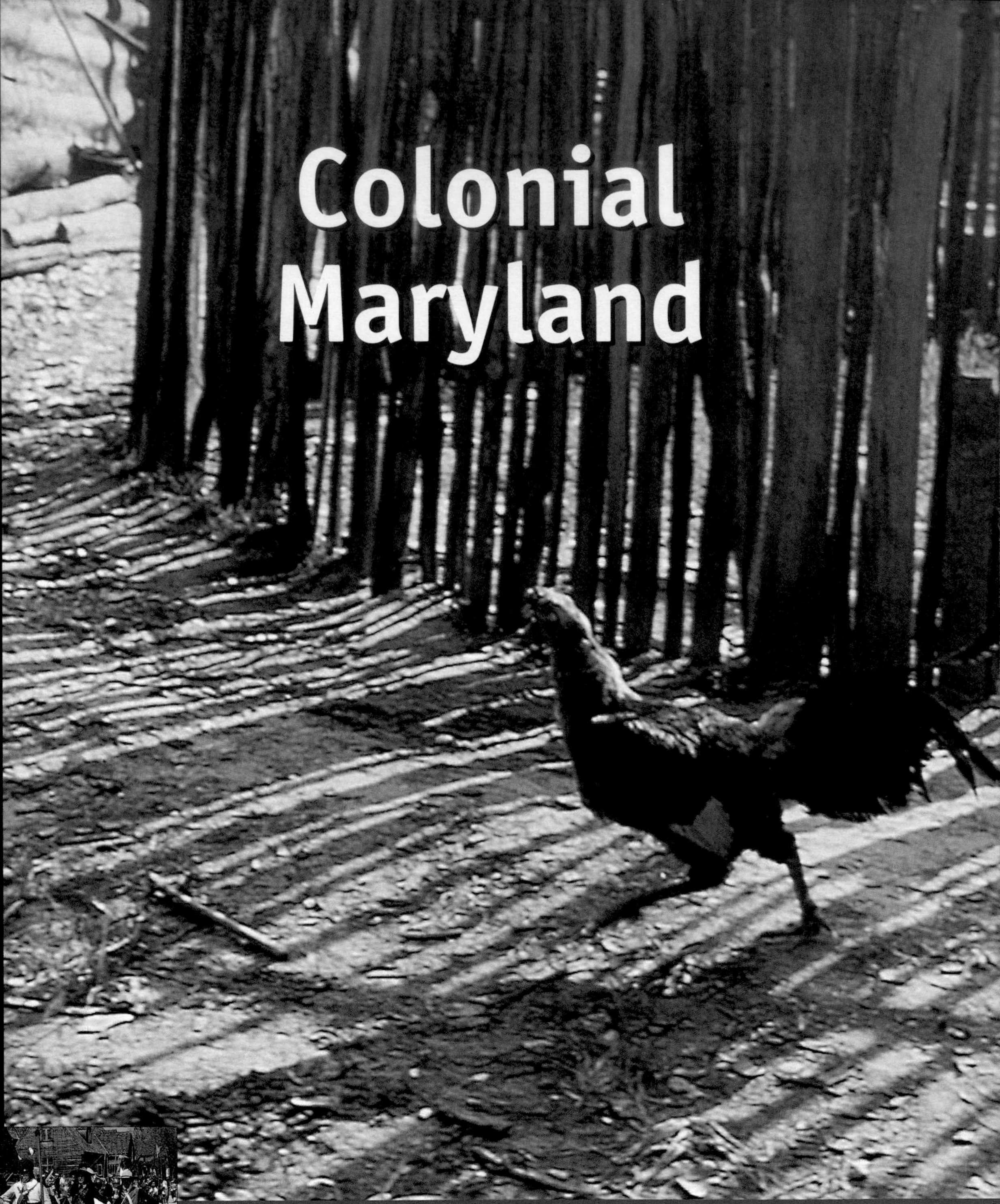

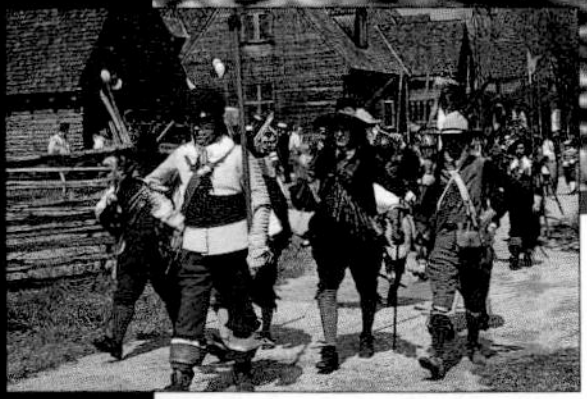

timeline of events

1590 · 1610 · 1630 · 1650

1607
Jamestown Colony is started in Virginia.

1608
Captain John Smith makes a map of the Chesapeake Bay.

1620
The Pilgrims land in Massachusetts. They start Plymouth Colony.

1624
New Amsterdam is settled.

1633
November 22
Colonists aboard the *Ark* and the *Dove* leave England for Maryland.

1634
March 25
The *Ark* and the *Dove* land on St. Clement's Island in the Potomac River.
St. Mary's City is founded.

chapter 3

Modern girls dressed in costume chase chickens on a colonial farm.

1689
Anglican (Protestant) leaders take over the government.

1694
The capital is moved to Annapolis.

1729
The town of Baltimore is started.

1670	1690	1710	1730	1750

1676
The Old State House is built in St. Mary's City.

1696
Maryland's first public school opens in Annapolis.

1649
The "Toleration Act" is passed.

51

EUROPEANS IN THE NEW WORLD

Who Was First?

Christopher Columbus sailed for the king and queen of Spain in 1492. Most people say he was the first European to see America. However, we know that sailors from Scandinavia, called Vikings, came to North America long before Columbus. Some people think that other ships from Europe, Africa, or Asia also crossed the Atlantic before Columbus.

EUROPEANS WERE BEGINNING to explore the world. They wanted to trade goods with people from other continents. They wanted to start *colonies*. The Portuguese first explored Africa and India. Soon Portuguese, Spanish, Dutch, Italian, English, and French explorers sailed to the Americas.

The explorers claimed to have discovered new lands. As you know, there were already people living in America. Many Europeans believed that the native people in the Americas and in Africa and India did not count because they looked different and had different religions. The Europeans felt they had the right to *conquer* people of different religions.

Many European countries claimed land in the Americas. In 1607, the English started a small colony in Virginia. They named it Jamestown, in honor of King James I. An English captain, John Smith, sailed from Jamestown up the Chesapeake Bay during the following year. He drew a map so that others could follow.

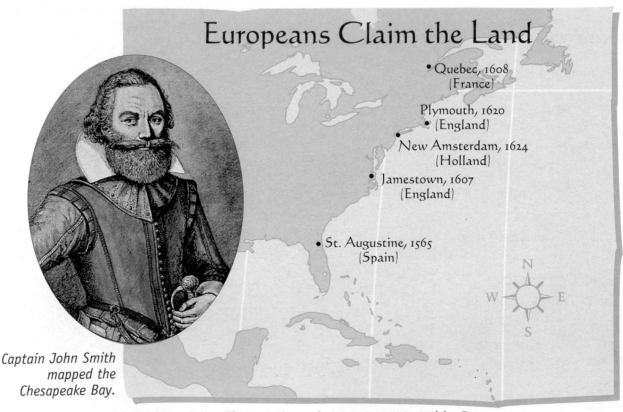

Captain John Smith mapped the Chesapeake Bay.

Europeans Claim the Land

• Quebec, 1608 (France)

Plymouth, 1620 • (England)

• New Amsterdam, 1624 (Holland)

• Jamestown, 1607 (England)

• St. Augustine, 1565 (Spain)

These early settlements were started by Europeans. Which colony was started first?

STARTING THE MARYLAND COLONY

The land that is now Maryland was *granted* by King Charles I of England to his friend George Calvert. The king also gave Calvert the title "Lord Baltimore."

Lord Baltimore was called the *proprietor* of his colony. He was given power in Maryland, just as the king had power in England. When George Calvert died, both the land and the title went to his son Cecilius.

Cecilius Calvert's brother Leonard came to be governor of the colony.

What do you think would be most important for the success of a new colony? If you said "good people," you are correct. Around 150 to 200 settlers came to Maryland on sailing ships from England.

Most of the people who sailed to Maryland left England because of problems there. When you understand their problems, you will know why they were willing to leave their homes and make such a dangerous trip.

Maryland was named after Queen Henrietta Marie.

Leonard Calvert was the first governor of the Maryland Colony.

Even though Cecilius Calvert was the proprietor, he never did come to Maryland. He stayed in England to take care of business there. Here he is shown with his grandson and a servant, who was also a child.

W h a t d o y o u t h i n k ?

Do you think it is fair to make someone give up his or her job because of religion?

This little piece of paper controlled a person's life for years.

Religious Troubles in Europe

In Europe, people were fighting over religion. Two groups were especially mad at each other. They were the Protestants and the Catholics. Protestants and Catholics had been fighting wars and killing each other for many years.

In some places, the ruler could choose one church and make everybody join. In England, the king had made himself head of the Church of England. If you did not belong to the Church of England, you were not considered a loyal subject of the king.

George Calvert had been raised as a Catholic in England. The king gave George Calvert an important government job. When George decided he wanted to practice the Catholic religion, he had to give up that job. No Catholics could vote or hold a government job. To make up for the lost job, King Charles I gave his friend land in America.

Calvert said there would not be one *official* church in Maryland. Both Catholics and Protestants could worship freely. Both could hold government jobs.

Money Troubles

There were other problems in Europe. Some people were very poor. The weather had been bad, and farm crops were ruined. Many people left their farms to move into the cities. But they could not find jobs, and they could not grow their own food in the city. They did not know how they would survive.

To make things worse, in those days people were put in jail if they owed money to someone and could not pay. Once a man or woman was in jail, it was impossible to earn money to pay off the *debt*.

The colonies in America offered a way out of trouble. Wealthy people in America paid the cost of the trip. Then, in exchange, poor people worked off the cost of the trip. They signed a contract called an indenture. It stated the number of years of work that were required. These people were called *indentured servants*. After the contract was up, indentured servants were free to look for new jobs. Men tried to save money to buy land.

Most of the people sailed on the larger ship, the Ark. A small crew brought supplies on the Dove. *Today, you can visit a **replica** of the Dove in St. Mary's City.*

THE VOYAGE OF THE *ARK* AND THE *DOVE*

Two small sailing ships, named the *Ark* and the *Dove*, sailed into the Chesapeake Bay. After four long months at sea, they had finally arrived in Maryland.

The ships stopped first at a small island in the Potomac River. The settlers named it St. Clement's Island.

Every man, woman, and child was glad the trip was over. Two storms had terrified them. The winds blew so hard and the waves rose so high that all the passengers were afraid their ship would sink. They were also afraid of a pirate attack. About twelve people died of a fever during the trip. Sailing the sea was dangerous.

The trip was also very uncomfortable. A few wealthy gentlemen had cabins, but most of the people lived all together on the lower deck. They ate and slept there. They had no privacy. Their bedding, spread out on the deck floor, was often wet. You can imagine how glad everyone was to get off the ship.

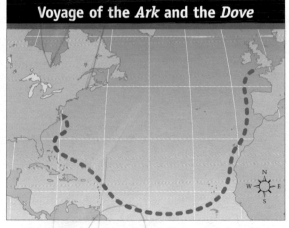

Voyage of the *Ark* and the *Dove*

The Ark *and the* Dove *left England at the end of November. They arrived in Maryland at the end of March. We celebrate the day the colonists landed at St. Clement's Island as Maryland Day.*

Passengers on the Ark and the Dove

Who came to Maryland on the *Ark* and the *Dove*? Most of the passengers, as well as all the crew, were men. Very few women and children came. Most of the men were English. A few were rich Catholics. Most of the passengers were poor men. Many of them owed money in England. Two African men came on the *Ark*.

Leonard Calvert was only twenty-three years old when he was named governor of Maryland. Because he was Catholic, he had no political rights in England. In Maryland he did have political power. He could own land and become wealthy.

Thomas Cornwallis was also from a Catholic family. He paid his own way. He was given land just for coming. For every servant he brought, Cornwallis was given more land. He could get rich very quickly this way.

Father Andrew White was one of two Catholic priests. At fifty-four, he was the oldest passenger. He wrote a book about starting the colony. He worked to convert the Indians to Christianity.

Mathias de Sousa was one of two Africans on board. He was an indentured servant who worked for Father White. Later, he piloted a boat and traded for furs with the Indians. He voted in the colonial assembly along with the other free men in the colony.

William Browne was only ten years old. He was an indentured servant of Thomas Cornwallis. He had to work as a servant until he was eighteen. At first, he gathered firewood and hauled water. When he grew older, he could do heavy farm and building work. After he became free, he became a farmer.

- Would you like to be an indentured servant like young William Browne?
- Do you think that ten-year-old children should work?
- What do children that age do today?

What kinds of things to you see in this corner of the Dove? What might they have been used for?

> . . . wee came into Chesapeake Bay, and made sayle to the North for Patoemeck river. . . . It is one of the delightfullest waters I ever saw. . . . And now being in our owne Countrey, wee began to give names to places. . .
>
> —*Father Andrew White*

The Maryland Adventure

MARYLAND'S FIRST TOWN

The people who came on the *Ark* and the *Dove* had to choose a place to live. St. Clement's Island was too small. They picked land where the Yaocomico [yow COM ih co] Indians already had a village. The English gave the Indians cloth, hatchets, and hoes in exchange for the right to settle on the land.

The Yaocomicos were helpful to the settlers. They let them live in their wigwams. They gave them corn and other foods to eat. They taught them to plant corn, beans, and squash together. They taught them what herbs made good medicines. They showed them where to find oysters and clams.

The settlers put up a high wooden fence. They built houses. Most houses had only one room and a dirt floor. Because it was spring, they could begin farming. They planted fields just outside the village.

The settlers called their town St. Mary's City. It was the colony's first capital.

Men guarded the new town. After some years, people began to build larger homes like the ones in the background.

St. Mary's City

St. Clement's Island

St. Mary's City was built next to an Indian village. Can you see longhouses outside the fence?

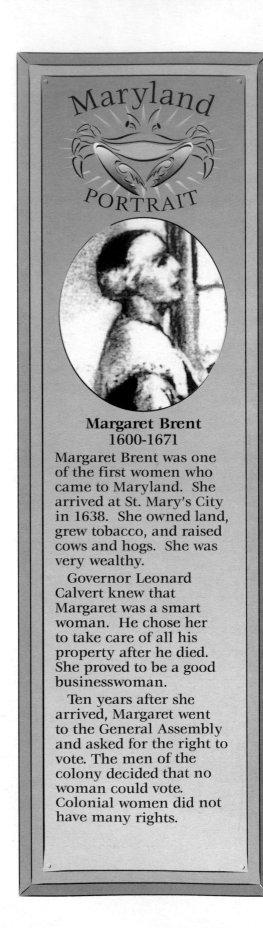
THE COLONY GROWS

Other settlers soon joined the passengers of the *Ark*. They brought more indentured servants. The colony needed many workers to help clear land, plant crops, and build houses. Women began to join the men here. Children were born. Instead of being mostly men, Maryland became home to many families. They quickly settled land all along both sides of the Chesapeake Bay.

People grew their own food. They grew corn and vegetables. They raised cows and hogs. The Indians introduced the settlers to tobacco. The settlers grew the plant and sold the leaves to buyers in England. They called it "the stinking weed."

Tobacco became the major crop in the colony.

Tobacco was too bulky to carry very far across the land, where there were no real roads. So the farmers spread out along the rivers, where boats could come to pick up their crops. The same boats brought goods from England. They brought cloth, tools, and other things that were not available here. Trading goods was an important way to make money.

Changing the Environment

All the new people and their ways of farming changed the natural environment. Tobacco is a plant that uses up a lot of the nutrients in the soil. After four years or so, farmers had to plant in new fields. This meant that forests had to be cleared.

Without forests to hold the soil in place, mud flowed into creeks and rivers. The mud, or *silt*, killed fish and shellfish. It made some rivers so shallow that large ships could no longer sail in them.

Changing Life for American Indians

As the forests were destroyed, Indians could not live as they had before. There were fewer animals to hunt. There was less land on which the Indians could plant crops. The Indian people could no longer meet their own needs.

Soon Indian people began to buy things like clothes, food, and tools from the colonists. The Indians came to rely on these things.

Europeans brought new diseases to America. Many Indians died of smallpox, measles, and other diseases. As their land disappeared and their people died, many Piscataways and Nanticokes moved away from the colonists. Only a few remained in their *traditional* homes.

▼ Drawing by Gary Rasmussen

Indian people traded furs for clothing, metal tools, and food.

THE BEGINNINGS OF SLAVERY

A ship carrying thirteen Africans arrived at St. Mary's City in 1642. Other ships followed. Some Africans came with indenture papers and became free. But others were captured and brought to Maryland as *slaves*.

Years later, Maryland passed a law saying that Africans without indenture papers were slaves for life. It said that the children of slaves would also be slaves for life. Even children had to work all day, usually in the tobacco fields.

This was the beginning of the very cruel system of slavery in Maryland. Human beings were treated as property. They were bought and sold. Slaves had to work their whole lives without any pay. The owners could whip their slaves if they wanted to.

Children and parents could be sold to different owners. They might never see each other again. Parents could not protect their children.

> ## **W** h a t   d o   y o u   t h i n k **?**
>
> Describe the feelings you might have had if you were a slave child.
> - What things would you have been afraid of?
> - What things would you have wanted to do that you could not do?

When the ships landed, slave families were split apart and sold to different owners.

EVERYDAY LIFE IN COLONIAL MARYLAND

When you look around our state today, you can see many different kinds of people. There are men, women, and children. There are rich folks and poor folks, and a lot of people in between. Some people were born here, and others came here from another country. Our ancestors came from many different places.

The same was true in colonial Maryland, although there was not as much variety as we have now. Maryland had grown a lot since the settlers first arrived. Let's learn about the people who lived in Maryland around 1750.

Poplar Hill Plantation was in Prince George's County. By the middle of the 1700s, a few planters lived on large plantations such as this one. They had large houses, well-kept grounds, and their own docks. They depended on the work of slaves for their wealth.

The Gentry

The rich families usually owned *plantations*, or large farms. Some men had other businesses or were lawyers. The men from these families held the high government jobs. The women were in charge of home life. They ran the house and took care of the children. They provided medical care for everyone on the plantation.

Children of the upper class, or *gentry*, were educated. Often a tutor came to the house to teach the lessons.

Both boys and girls learned to read and write. Boys studied Latin and Greek. Some boys traveled to Europe for more education. Girls learned to sew and do needlework. Both boys and girls learned to play a musical instrument.

The gentry built large brick homes. Inside, they had furniture from England. They owned books, musical instruments, gold jewelry, and fine clothes. Wealthy families owned slaves and had servants.

What kinds of things do you see in the dining room at the elegant Hammond-Harwood House in Annapolis?

Families in the Middle

Many people were neither rich nor poor. They owned a home and some land. Some people had to rent land because they could not afford to buy it. Many worked at crafts. They were carpenters or cobblers (shoemakers). Their homes might have just one or two rooms. Most of their furniture and clothing was made in Maryland, although they often used English cloth.

Both men and women did a lot of their own work. The men worked in the fields and at their craft. The women made clothing, prepared the meals, took care of the garden, and made household items. Some families had one or several slaves or servants.

Both boys and girls helped with the family's work. Some children, especially boys, went to school. Indian and African children were not allowed in the schools.

When a family could afford it, they added to their small house. Why do you think this style of home is called a "telescope house"?

This kitchen and dining area belonged to Joseph Neall, a middle-class worker.

Hired Workers, Servants, and Slaves

Men and women who did not have the money to buy or rent land had to work for other people. They hoped to save enough money to buy land, but they were not always able to. Their houses were small. They made the furniture themselves.

Slaves were very important in building Maryland's *economy*. By the mid-1700s slaves grew much of the tobacco that made the colony a success. A few worked in the plantation owner's house cooking, cleaning, or taking care of children. Some learned skilled crafts such as carpentry or blacksmithing. The work of slaves made the land-owners very rich, but the slaves did not get any rewards for their hard work.

Not all black people were slaves. Some families had been free since the earliest colonial days. Some had become free. Many worked for wages. Some owned small farms or worked at skilled crafts. Children usually worked along with their parents because the families needed their pay. Some could read and write, although most of the children did not get to go to school.

Slaves were forced to work long hours in the fields. Children over seven had to work along with the grown-ups.

On large plantations, slaves lived in the slave quarters. Houses for slaves and indentured servants were small.

The Johnsons, a family of free blacks, moved from Virginia to Maryland in the 1660s. First they rented land. Later, John Johnson bought his own farm. He named the farm Angola.

COLONIAL TOWNS

At first, most people did not settle in towns. They were spread out on farms across the colony. Small towns grew up. Then, as more people settled in central Maryland, the capital was moved from St. Mary's City to Annapolis.

Annapolis

Annapolis was a port on the Chesapeake Bay. The town grew because it was the seat of government. The General Assembly met there. People came from all over Maryland to do business with the colonial government. Annapolis needed inns and restaurants for all these visitors.

Soon Annapolis was the colony's largest town. Lawyers and merchants lived there. Men and sometimes women ran shops. They sold food, paper goods, cloth, hats, shoes and boots, furniture, candles, clocks, and silver dishes and jewelry.

The colony's first newspaper, *The Maryland Gazette*, was published in Annapolis. Jonas Green was the first publisher. When he died, his wife Anne Catherine Green took over. She was also the "public printer." The government paid her to print all the official papers.

The towns of Oxford, Chestertown, Joppa, Port Tobacco, and Baltimore followed. All these towns were built near rivers and the bay. Ships from all the colonies and from England came to ports in the Chesapeake region. Men opened shipyards to build and repair boats. Port cities were busy places.

Some families built large homes in Annapolis.

King William's School

The first public school in Maryland was King William's School in Annapolis. The school was for white boys only. Students learned Greek, Latin, writing, and other subjects to prepare them for the new William and Mary College in Virginia.

ANNAPOLIS, *August* 22, 1765.

TO BE SOLD,

A LARGE New Topsail Schooner, Burthen 86 Tons, with all her Tackling and Apparel, as good as new, was built last Year, at *Liverpool*, in *Nova-Scotia*, and is a prime Sailer. Any Person inclinable to purchase, are desired to ap- ly to ELIZABETH RUTLAND.

This ad from The Maryland Gazette *is selling a large ship.*

The Maryland Adventure

Baltimore Town

At first, Baltimore was just farmland. Then Charles and Daniel Carroll of Annapolis sold some land so a town could be built on it. The new town was located on a good harbor. Roads were planned. The land was split into lots for people to buy.

Baltimore grew slowly. After twenty years it had only twenty-five houses, two taverns, one church, a tobacco warehouse, a barbershop, and an insurance office. Craftspeople worked at home.

A surveyor divided the land into lots to make Baltimore Town in 1729.

In this view of Baltimore in 1752 you can see St. Paul's Church on the hill. Two ships are anchored in the harbor. Just eight years later there were 200 homes and many more businesses.

MARYLAND'S FRONTIER

Settlers moved to the fertile hills and valleys in central and western Maryland. They grew wheat and some vegetables and fruits.

Wheat was very important in the history of Maryland. Most families growing wheat lived on small farms and did most of the work themselves. They usually did not have slaves or indentured servants.

Many towns, such as Baltimore and Chestertown, became centers for shipping wheat to other colonies. They also shipped wheat to the West Indies. The people who built and owned the sailing ships that carried wheat made good money.

Before the wheat could be shipped, it had to be made into flour. This was done at a mill. Mills cost a lot of money to build, but their owners could earn a good living. Towns developed along the fall line, where there was rushing water. The waterfalls provided power for the mills.

The wheat farmers needed towns as central places to sell or ship their wheat. They also needed mills to grind their wheat into flour. They needed stores where they could buy supplies that were sent from the East. Towns grew to meet the need for mills and stores.

Can you see the waterwheel at the Amos Mill in Norrisville?

▲ Photo by M.E. Warren

Western Towns

Onc important town was Frederick. A man named Daniel Dulany had bought a lot of land in western Maryland. He wanted to sell that land. He built a town to attract farmers. Dulany offered a good price to craftsmen and shopkeepers who moved thcre. The farmers followed. Frederick became the center of Maryland's frontier.

Thirty miles farther west, Jonathan Hager laid out a town on land that he owned. He was inspired by Frederick's success. Hager wanted to name his town after his wife Elizabeth, but people called it Hager's Town. The name stuck.

Mason-Dixon Line
• Hagerstown
• Frederick

The Mason-Dixon Line

Maryland and Pennsylvania disagreed for many years about the boundary between them. Finally, in 1763, the English government sent two surveyors to determine the border. Their names were Charles Mason and Jeremiah Dixon. The border was called the Mason-Dixon Line.

Mason and Dixon used stone markers to form the border. Many of the stone markers remain today.

Thomas Cresap

Thomas Cresap was a Maryland pioneer. He was one of the first colonial settlers to move into western Maryland. In the 1730s, he traded with the Shawnee Indians.

As other settlers followed, Cresap opened up a trading post. He sold salt, gunpowder, and cloth for sewing. He drew maps of the western lands and rivers which he knew well.

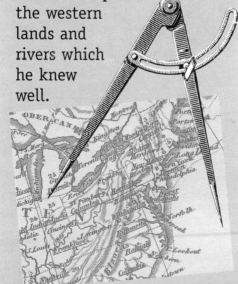

German farmers from Pennsylvania moved into Maryland. Many of them belonged to the Lutheran Church. The Scotch-Irish had moved from Scotland to Ireland and then to America. Most of them were Presbyterians.

The Toleration Act

Today, in the United States, every person is free to choose a religion. Each religion can have a building where people worship. Members of all religions can vote. This was not always so.

Maryland was the first colony to make a law that said people had to **tolerate** different religions. In 1649, the General Assembly voted in favor of the "Toleration Act."

The act said that all people would be free to practice their own religion. It set punishments for anyone who called people of other religions by bad names. But there was one big problem with this law. It was for Christians only. Jews and others were not protected by this law.

The Toleration Act did not last. Maryland soon returned to religious **discrimination**. It would be many years before the troubles ended.

RELIGION AND GOVERNMENT

Another war over religion began in England in the 1640s. People in Maryland and Virginia started to fight, too. One group of Protestants was the Puritans. For a while, Puritans controlled the colony.

Time passed, and the different religious groups still had problems. Once again, those troubles spilled over into Maryland. In the end, the conflict was solved by a *compromise*. The Calvert family became Protestants. They joined the Church of England. Again they were allowed to govern the colony.

The Church of England became the official church in Maryland. That meant that everyone, no matter what their religion, had to pay taxes to support that church. Quakers could no longer be members of the General Assembly. Catholics could not worship in public. They were not allowed to build churches.

Saint Paul's Episcopal Church was in Baltimore.

Voting in the Colony

The General Assembly was made up of men who were elected to make laws for the colony. However, not everyone was allowed to vote. A person had to own property in order to vote. Later, only Protestants could vote. Catholics could not vote. Jews could not vote. Colonial Maryland never did stop people from voting because of their race. However, only a few blacks owned enough property to vote. Women could not vote at all in colonial Maryland.

The Maryland Adventure

Different Classes

Draw pictures in which you show how different classes of people in colonial Maryland lived. Show them at home and at work. Draw someone from a wealthy family, someone from a middle-class farm family, and someone from a slave or servant family. See how much you can show about their lives in the pictures you draw. Use the photos in this chapter to help you get ideas.

Questions for Review

1. How did Maryland get its name?

2. Who was Maryland's first proprietor? What was his son's name? What was their religion?

3. What were two problems of life in Europe?

4. Name the two ships that brought the first colonists to Maryland.

5. What was Maryland's first town and first capital?

6. Name a woman from colonial Maryland. What did she do?

7. What were two important crops that grew in colonial Maryland?

8. What were two ways life changed for American Indians after the colonists came?

9. Rich families that owned plantations were called the _____.

10. Name three kinds of work done by slaves.

11. What town was Maryland's second capital?

12. Name at least three groups of people who could not vote in Maryland in 1750.

13. What was Maryland's "Toleration Act"? Did it include everyone?

Geography Tie-In

1. Why did the early colonists want to live by rivers?

2. Why was the Atlantic Coastal Plain region settled first?

3. Give three examples of how the colonists changed the natural environment.

chapter 4

THE TIME
1750–1800

PEOPLE TO KNOW
George Washington
Zachariah Hood
Anthony Stewart
Thomas Jefferson
Mary Katherine
 Goddard
Charles Carroll
Samuel Chase
William Paca
Thomas Stone
General Lafayette
General Cornwallis
Thomas Johnson Jr.
Andrew Ellicott
Benjamin Banneker

PLACES TO LOCATE
England
Thirteen Colonies
Canada
Mississippi River
Appalachian Mountains
Boston, Massachusetts
Annapolis
Philadelphia,
 Pennsylvania
Concord, Massachusetts
Lexington,
 Massachusetts
Frederick
Yorktown, Virginia
Potomac River
Washington, D.C.

70

timeline of events

1750

1755

1760

1765
The Stamp Act is passed.

1765

1773
The Tea Act is passed.
Boston Tea Party

1754–1763
French and Indian War

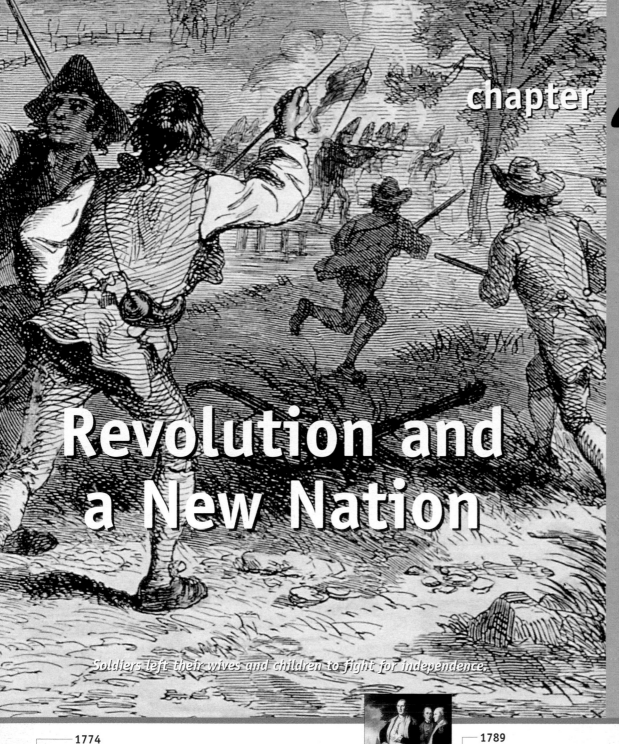

Soldiers left their wives and children to fight for independence.

chapter

4

TERMS TO UNDERSTAND

empire
militia
tax
representative
protest
resist
rebellious
cooperate
revolution
import
Loyalist
Patriot
ammunition
independence
treason
impel
barracks
ironworks
privateer
ideal
amendment
survey

Revolution and a New Nation

1774
First Continental Congress meets.

1776
July 4
The Declaration of Independence is signed.

1789
The U.S. Constitution is approved.
In Baltimore, an anti-slavery society is started.

1800
Congress meets in the new U.S. Capitol
for the first time.

| 1775 | 1780 | 1785 | 1790 | 1795 | |

1775–1783
War for Independence

1784
A law says that Maryland cannot import slaves anymore.

1790
Maryland gives land for the nation's
capital, Washington, D.C.

ON THE FRONTIER

BY THE MID 1700S, England had thirteen colonies in North America. Maryland and the other colonies were part of the British *Empire*, or kingdom. In this chapter you will read about how the colonies became states and formed the new United States of America.

England is part of Great Britain. English people are also called British.

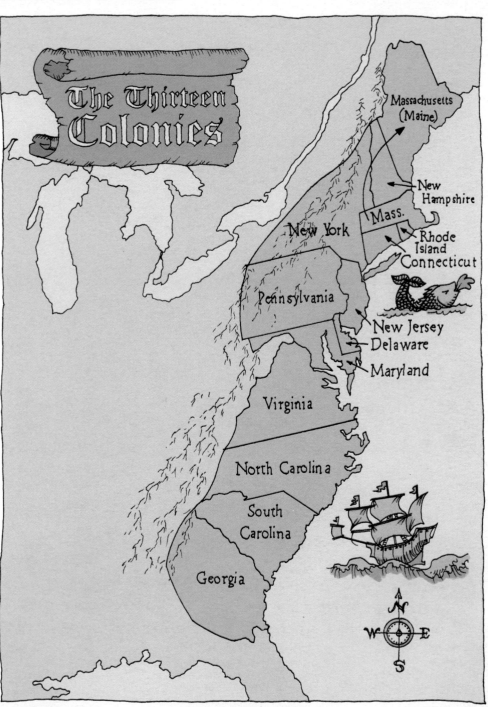

The Thirteen Colonies

Massachusetts (Maine)

New Hampshire

New York

Mass.

Rhode Island

Connecticut

Pennsylvania

New Jersey

Delaware

Maryland

Virginia

North Carolina

South Carolina

Georgia

▲ Drawing by Gary Rasmussen

The Maryland Adventure

Modern men show how colonial men loaded a cannon at Fort Frederick.

Fighting for the Frontier

While England had its thirteen colonies, France controlled the land around the colonies. Both England and France wanted their empires to grow. They went to war over the land.

The Indians also wanted the land. It was their home. They had been giving furs to the French in exchange for metal knives, guns, and cooking pots. The Indians helped the French fight the British.

England got men from the thirteen colonies to help fight France. The colonists called this the French and Indian War, because they were fighting both the French and the Indians.

Important Results for America

After seven years, England won the war. They won control of land in Canada and all the way west to the Mississippi River.

American men had gained military experience. They had practiced fighting in colonial *militias*, or armies. Men like George Washington had learned to command troops. Colonial assemblies had helped the people organize and pay for the war. These things were important for what was about to happen.

George Washington got lots of good military experience during the French and Indian War.

EARLY SIGNS OF TROUBLE

The British did not want to fight any more Indian wars, so they told the colonists not to move west of the Appalachian Mountains. But some colonists had already bought land there. They wanted to be able to go to that land.

The British also wanted the colonists to pay for the war. It had cost a lot of money.

The colonists believed that they had already paid. They had given men and supplies. But England decided to *tax* the colonists to raise money. They made new rules that made the colonists very angry.

The Stamp Act

One tax the British made the colonists pay was called the Stamp Act. It said the colonists had to buy stamps to put on all kinds of papers. Business and legal papers, marriage licenses, wills, newspapers, and even playing cards had to have stamps. If they did not have stamps, the documents were not legal.

An Annapolis merchant named Zachariah Hood, who was in England at the time, took the job of stamp collector for Maryland. When he returned to Maryland, a mob tore down his warehouse where the stamps were stored. Hood fled to New York.

Maryland's General Assembly met to discuss the Stamp Act. The men agreed that England did not have the right to tax the colonists. The colonists were not allowed to send *representatives* to Parliament (the lawmaking group in London). Because of this, many colonists thought Parliament should not be allowed to tax them. They felt it was unfair to be taxed when they had no say.

The rallying cry became "No taxation without representation!" Some men formed a group to *protest* the taxes. The group was called the Sons of Liberty.

The colonists protested so much that the British took away the Stamp Act. The colonists learned important lessons from this. They learned that if they *resisted*, the British would back down. They also learned how to organize and protest.

The colonists argued with the British over the Stamp Act.

This newspaper drawing was about the Stamp Act. The skull and crossbones are signs of danger. The words say that the times are "dreadful, dismal, doleful, dolorous, and dollar-less." Look up "doleful" and "dolorous" in a dictionary to see what they mean.

The TIMES are Dreadful, Dismal, Doleful, Dolorous, and DOLLAR-LESS.

The Tea Act

The British put a tax on tea. Tea, a popular drink, was shipped to America on British ships. The British also tried to force the colonists to buy tea from the British East India Company. Once again, the colonists resisted.

The first protest was in Massachusetts. In Boston, men dressed up like American Indians and went to the harbor. They went on board a British ship and dumped all the tea into the water. Robert Sessions wrote down what happened in his diary:

> *The chests were . . . opened, the tea emptied over the side, and the chests thrown overboard. . . . Although there were many people on the wharf, [there was] entire silence. . . .*

This event is called the Boston Tea Party.

In towns in many colonies, women organized the Daughters of Liberty. They refused to buy tea. They shared recipes for other drinks. Because women were in charge of buying food, this was a very important action.

Other Problems Grow

The colonists had other complaints about the British. They complained about paying taxes that were used for the Church of England. Everyone's tax money went to support that one church. Catholics, Presbyterians, Lutherans, Quakers, and Jews had to pay the tax. Many people did not think it was fair.

The colonists grew more and more *rebellious*. They didn't want to take orders from rulers who lived over 3,000 miles away on the other side of the Atlantic Ocean.

Marylanders also protested the Tea Act. When a ship named the Peggy Stewart *arrived in Annapolis carrying tea, some people were very angry. The ship's owner, Anthony Stewart, feared for his life. To protect himself and his family from harm, Stewart burned his own ship. An excited crowd watched as it burned. Everyone could see how powerful the protesters had become.*
(Painting by Francis Blackwell Mayer)

THE COLONISTS COME TOGETHER

Men from all across the colonies met in Philadelphia, Pennsylvania, to talk about their problems with the British. The men used words like "liberty" and "rights" as they talked with each other. They said they wanted liberty from British laws that hurt them. They said the laws and taxes were hurting the American economy. They said that Americans should have more rights. They agreed to stop trading with England until they could get what they wanted.

The men from all the colonies began to work together. They got to know each other. They learned how to *cooperate*.

A revolution is when people fight to replace one government with a different government.

Marylanders Come Together

At home, men from all across Maryland met in Annapolis. They called this meeting the Convention. The members of the Convention began to make laws for Maryland.

At the Convention, every free man in Maryland was asked to sign an oath of loyalty to the revolutionary government. Then everyone could know who supported the *revolution* and who wanted to stay with England. Everyone could know who could serve in the militia when the fighting started.

Annapolis

Across the Colonies

In Massachusetts, after the Boston Tea Party, England had closed down the port. Everyone who sold or shipped things out of Boston could no longer make a living. Nothing could be shipped into Boston, either. Massachusetts *imported* a lot of its food from colonies further south. The people would be hungry if they could not get food. Maryland and the other colonies were very angry about what the British had done to Boston. They joined together to send supplies to that city.

Colonists who did not want to break away from England were called *Loyalists*. Colonists who supported the Revolution were called *Patriots*.

In Virginia and some other colonies, British rules were hurting the tobacco trade. Also, the British told some of the colonial assemblies that they could no longer meet. Southern planters were just as angry as the townspeople of Boston were.

Across the colonies, people began collecting guns and *ammunition* to get ready for whatever would happen next. At the same time, England was sending more soldiers and ships to America. They would be ready if fighting broke out.

Colonists and British soldiers met at Concord Bridge. Americans called the British soldiers "Redcoats" or "Lobster-Backs." Why do you think they chose these names?

THE FIGHTING BEGINS

The first battles took place in Massachusetts. A British general sent troops to take away the weapons and ammunition that colonists had collected in a town called Concord. When the British reached Lexington, on the way to Concord, they were met by armed men from the local militia.

Shots were fired. Then there was more shooting in Concord and later on the road back to Boston. Men on both sides were killed. This was the beginning of the Revolutionary War, or the War for Independence.

AMERICA DECLARES INDEPENDENCE

Once the American and British soldiers were at war, more Americans demanded *independence*. Men from all the colonies met again in Philadelphia.

The men voted to declare independence from England. For two days, Thomas Jefferson of Virginia and several other men worked on the exact words to use in a letter to the king. On July 4, 1776, the Declaration of Independence was signed.

The men who voted for independence were committing *treason*. Treason is a crime against the government. The British government could sentence them to death. What they did was very risky and very brave. The men believed that what they did was right. They believed it was worth the risk.

Thomas Jefferson drafted the Declaration of Independence.

The Declaration of Independence

When in the course of human events, it becomes necessary for one people to dissolve the political bonds which have connected them with another . . . they should declare the causes which **impel** *them to the separation.*

We hold these truths to be self-evident: That all men are created equal; that they are endowed by their creator with certain unalienable rights; that among these are life, liberty, and the pursuit of happiness; that to secure these rights, governments are instituted among men, deriving their just powers from the consent of the governed; that whenever any form of government becomes destructive of these ends, it is the right of the people to alter or to abolish it . . .

These words begin one of the most famous documents in the history of the world. Because the Declaration of Independence was written over 200 years ago, the language is a little hard to understand. Here is the meaning in modern language:

The first part says that the writers are going to explain why the colonies are declaring independence from British rule. The colonists felt that they were taking such an important step that they should tell everyone why they were doing it.

The second part begins the explanation. It says that all men are born with certain rights. These rights include life, liberty, and the pursuit of happiness. Governments are supposed to protect these rights. If a government does not protect the rights of the people, then the people can get rid of that government and start a new one.

The Declaration also says that all governments get their power from the people. That is why the people can and should change their government if it is hurting them.

Next, the Declaration lists the ways in which the British government had been hurting the colonists. In all, the Declaration of Independence lists twenty-seven ways in which the British harmed the colonists.

At the end of the list, Jefferson wrote that all these things meant that the colonists were right to go to war. It was right because the British had harmed, not protected, the colonists.

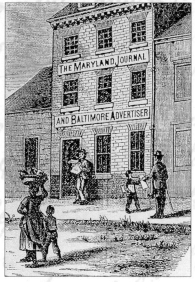

The Maryland Journal and Baltimore Advertiser *was a newspaper that ran stories about the Revolution. It published the Declaration of Independence so that all Marylanders could read it.*

Mary Katherine Goddard published the newspaper. She was also in charge of Baltimore's mail.

Four Men from Maryland Signed the Declaration of Independence

Charles Carroll was born in Annapolis. He became a lawyer. He was active in protests before the Revolution. After the war, he served in the Maryland State Senate and the U.S. Senate. He was the only Roman Catholic signer of the Declaration of Independence.

Samuel Chase was born in Somerset County. His father did not have a lot of money, but he gave Samuel a good education. Samuel studied law. After the war, he became a U.S. Supreme Court Justice.

William Paca was born in Harford County. He was also a lawyer. After the war he served in the Maryland General Assembly, as governor of Maryland, and as a judge.

Thomas Stone, born in Charles County, was a lawyer like the other Maryland signers. He served in the General Assembly. He died young, some say because of his grief over the death of his wife a few months earlier.

THE WAR FOR INDEPENDENCE

General George Washington led the American troops. He was an excellent commander. Maryland's soldiers were some of the best he had. They fought in New York, New Jersey, Pennsylvania, Virginia, North Carolina, and South Carolina.

Maryland was lucky that no major battles were fought here. There was a lot of action, however, on the Chesapeake Bay. Both the Americans and the British sent ships there. When the armies left the ships to march across the land, they often stole from local farms to get food and firewood.

Marylanders Do Their Part

Many Marylanders left their families and jobs to join the militia. They made great sacrifices to fight for independence. They risked their lives. Sometimes they did not have uniforms or enough ammunition. Sometimes they were not paid.

Maryland's government chose the army officers. Usually they were from the gentry. Farmers, craftsmen, and shopkeepers fought as soldiers.

African Americans, both slave and free, fought in the war. Black and white men who knew the bay were pilots on ships that patrolled the Chesapeake. Their skill and knowledge of the bay helped to win the war.

German settlers fought too. For the first time, the German settlers were considered Americans. The war was an opportunity for different kinds of people to get to know each other and work together.

The Breadbasket of the Revolution

Maryland's wheat fed many soldiers and sailors. The trade in grain brought a lot of business to Maryland merchants and ship owners. The port of Baltimore grew during the war.

Other products from Maryland were also used in the war. Maryland's *ironworks* made cannons. Shipyards built many of the ships used by the American navy.

*Some American soldiers lived in **barracks** such as these in Frederick. Others had to camp out where they were fighting.*

This cow's horn was used to carry gunpowder and keep it dry.

▲ Photo by Jean Crossman, Courtesy of the Amherst History Museum

Privateers

Ship captains from Maryland became *privateers*. They attacked and captured enemy ships. They also took the cargo from British ships. They got to keep what they captured. Some privateers became quite rich this way.

Help from the French

The colonies had good help in the Revolution. France sent soldiers to help the colonists. (Remember, France and Britain were enemies.) The French General Lafayette was very popular in America, especially in Maryland.

VICTORY!

The last battle was at Yorktown, Virginia. American troops, including men from Maryland, defeated the British there. The British General Cornwallis ordered his men to hand over their weapons. The War for Independence had lasted for over six years.

The Americans had won. Now they really would be independent.

Results of the Revolution

A lot had changed after six years of war. The thirteen colonies could have their own government. People could move west of the Appalachian Mountains if they wanted to. British laws could no longer stop them.

There were other results, too. Many of the soldiers had traveled far away from their homes. They met different kinds of people from all across the states. Black and white men had fought together. Many slaves won their freedom by fighting in the Revolution.

General Washington stands at Yorktown. General Lafayette and Washington's chief aide, Lieutenant Colonel Tench Tilghman, are with him. Tilghman was from Maryland.

After the fighting was over, General Washington told Congress that he would become an ordinary citizen again.

Washington Steps Down

George Washington had done such a wonderful job as commander in chief of the army that some people wanted to make him king. Washington did not want to be king. He believed that the people should choose a president in an election.

Just before Christmas in 1783, the Congress was meeting in Annapolis. Washington came to the new State House to tell the men that he was leaving his military job. He would go home to Virginia as an ordinary citizen.

This was a very important event in our history. It set a pattern for the new country. From that time on, our presidents were elected. No general, however popular, ever tried to take over the office of president. Our government would be run by regular citizens, not by the army.

The Maryland Adventure

FORMING A NEW GOVERNMENT

With independence came a big job. That was to make the new nation work. Leaders turned their attention to building our country. They had a lot to do. They had to start a new government.

Maryland's State Government

The colonies had to set up governments as soon as they declared independence. Leaders in Maryland wrote a new state constitution in 1776. It said what offices there would be. It said what powers the government had and how laws would be made. It said who could vote in elections.

The governor was the highest state leader. Thomas Johnson Jr. was Maryland's first governor. The General Assembly had two parts—the State Senate and the House of Delegates. These two groups would make laws for the state.

The state constitution also said who could vote in the state. Today, as you know, every adult citizen can vote. Back then, only men could vote, and those men had to own property and be Christians. Poor men could not vote. Women could not vote. Slaves could not vote. American Indians could not vote. Jews could not vote.

A few free black men who owned property could vote in Maryland. Some ran for office, but they did not win. Roman Catholics once again had the right to vote.

This certainly was not a democracy as we think of it today. What had happened to the words "all men are created equal" that were written in the Declaration of Independence?

What Thomas Jefferson wrote in the Declaration of Independence described the world the way it should be. It was an *ideal* for people to try to live up to. Sometimes it is very difficult to make ideals become real.

Thomas Johnson Jr. was the first governor of the state of Maryland.

State leaders met at the State House in Annapolis.

Linking the past to the present

To start a new government was a difficult thing. Make a list of all the things that the government does today. Make another list of some of the people who work for the government. Is your list long enough to show you that the government has a really big job?

Benjamin Banneker
1731–1806

Benjamin Banneker was a free black man from Baltimore County. He was a farmer who taught himself math and science.

Benjamin built a wooden clock that kept perfect time. He kept beehives to get honey and did scientific studies of the bees.

Benjamin also studied the stars. He wrote down the movements of the moon and planets in an almanac. His almanac came out each year. He sent the first one to Thomas Jefferson.

In a letter, Banneker told Jefferson that slavery was wrong. He showed many people what African Americans could achieve if they were not kept in slavery.

The Constitution of the United States

Leaders from the states got together and wrote the Constitution of the United States of America. These are the laws that still guide our country 200 years later. We will learn more about our government in a later chapter.

A Bill of Rights

After the Constitution was written, the leaders wanted an extra guarantee that the new government could not stomp on the people's rights. They added ten *amendments* to the Constitution. These amendments are called the Bill of Rights.

The Bill of Rights guarantees us our precious freedoms. It lists the freedom of speech, freedom of the press, freedom of religion, the right to a trial by a jury if we are accused of a crime, and other important rights.

MARYLAND IN THE NEW NATION

Maryland took its place as one of the first thirteen states of the United States of America. One important task was to build a capital city for the nation. Maryland, like the other states, hoped to win this honor. In fact, Maryland was selected. Our state gave land for the new city on the banks of the Potomac River.

The place was chosen because it was in between the northern and southern states. That way it would not be too far from any state. It was named Washington, in honor of George Washington. Because the new city was not a state, but a special district for the government, it was called the District of Columbia, or D.C.

Before the government could move to Washington, D.C., the city had to be designed and the buildings put up. A Marylander named Andrew Ellicott *surveyed* the land where the city would be built. He was helped by another Marylander, Benjamin Banneker.

Liberty and Justice for ALL?

Many people freed their slaves because of the ideas of liberty from the Revolution. States north of Maryland passed laws to end slavery. Maryland did not end slavery, but many African Americans did become free.

Choose one freedom that is guaranteed in the Bill of Rights. Draw a picture of people using that freedom.

Questions for Review

1. What two European countries wanted to control the land west of the Appalachian Mountains?

2. Name the war fought over that land. Who won?

3. How do we know that the colonists did not like the Stamp Act and the Tea Act?

4. Where did the first battles of the War for Independence take place?

5. Why do we celebrate July 4 as Independence Day?

6. Name the four men from Maryland who signed the Declaration of Independence.

7. Who led the American troops during the War for Independence?

8. What contributions did Maryland make to the war?

9. What country helped colonists win the war?

10. Who was the first governor of the state of Maryland?

11. What do we call the written document that is the basis of our United States government?

12. What did Benjamin Banneker do for the new nation?

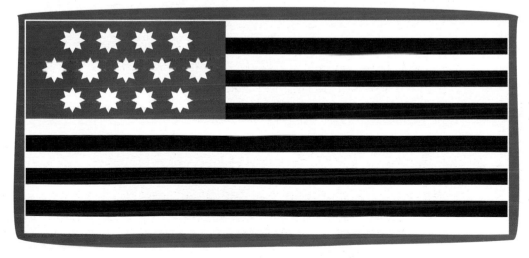

John Shaw was a cabinetmaker from Annapolis. He made two flags for the meeting of the Congress. You can see that there are thirteen stars and thirteen stripes for the original thirteen states. How is our flag different today?

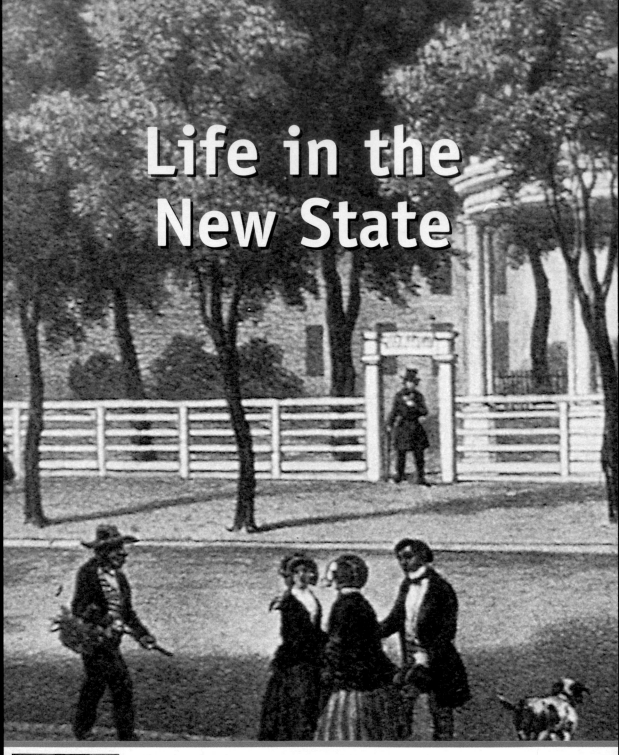

Life in the New State

timeline of events

1800

1810

1820

1812–1814
War of 1812

1818
The National Road opens from Cumberland to Wheeling, Virginia.

1814
The Battle of Baltimore
Francis Scott Key writes "The Star-Spangled Banner."

Vandalia

St. Louis

Illinois

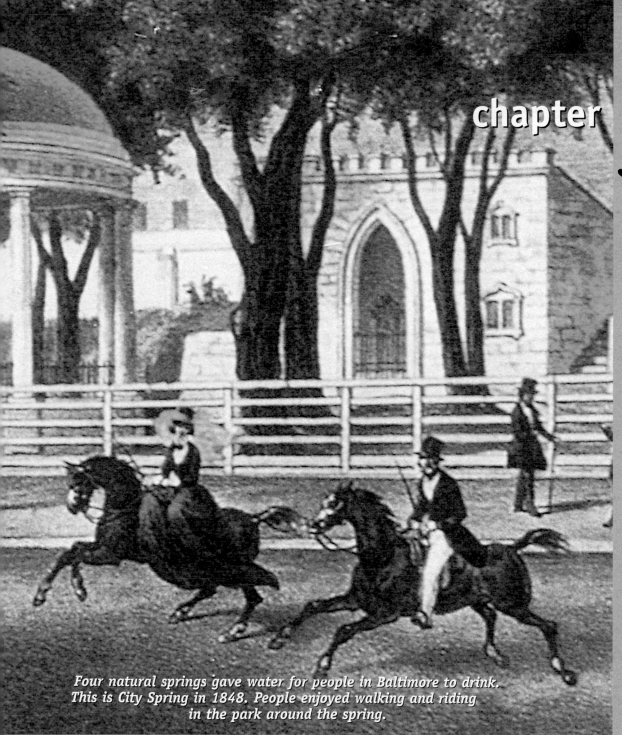

TERMS TO UNDERSTAND
industry
diverse
military
retreat
anthem
immigrant
almanac
congregation
ordain
saint

Four natural springs gave water for people in Baltimore to drink. This is City Spring in 1848. People enjoyed walking and riding in the park around the spring.

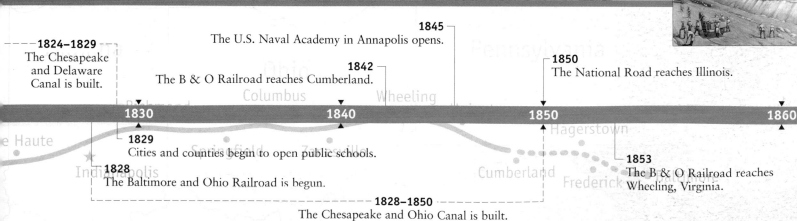

1845
The U.S. Naval Academy in Annapolis opens.

1824–1829
The Chesapeake and Delaware Canal is built.

1842
The B & O Railroad reaches Cumberland.

1850
The National Road reaches Illinois.

1830   **1840**   **1850**   **1860**

1829
Cities and counties begin to open public schools.

1828
The Baltimore and Ohio Railroad is begun.

1853
The B & O Railroad reaches Wheeling, Virginia.

1828–1850
The Chesapeake and Ohio Canal is built.

87

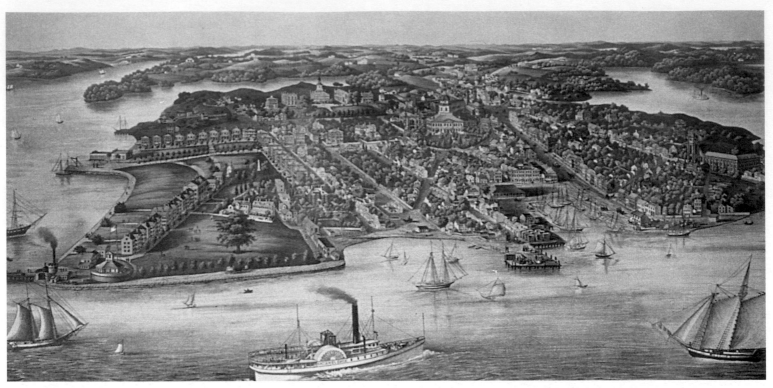

Annapolis continued to grow. Navy officers were trained at the new U.S. Naval Academy there.

CHANGES ACROSS THE LAND

Maryland grew after the American Revolution. Many different kinds of people lived in our new state. Each part of Maryland was changing in its own way.

Southern Maryland

Most people in southern Maryland were still farmers. Many grew tobacco. Many farmers did all their own work. A few wealthy people with a lot of land had slaves to do the hard work. Most African Americans in southern Maryland were slaves at this time.

The Eastern Shore

Most people on the Eastern Shore were farmers. Family members shared the work on most farms. They grew wheat and other crops.

Some farmers freed their slaves because they no longer needed them. Other people freed their slaves because they believed that slavery was wrong. Many free African Americans were farmers or farm workers.

Craftsmen made everything from shoes to furniture. A lot of men worked in shipyards. They made and repaired ships. Others worked on the water. They harvested seafood, especially oysters that lived in the Chesapeake Bay and in rivers near the bay.

Easton became the most important town on the Eastern Shore. The state government opened offices there.

Western Maryland

Western Maryland was no longer the frontier. Farms spread across the fertile valleys. People from other parts of Maryland moved there. Families coming to Maryland from other countries also settled there. There were settlers from Germany. The Scotch-Irish came too. They had moved from Scotland to Ireland and then to America.

This glass sugar bowl was made at the Amelung Glass Factory near Frederick.

Pioneers moving west wanted to buy glass and heavy iron tools in towns like Frederick and Hagerstown. Then they did not have to carry the goods as far as they would if they had bought them in eastern towns.

Central Maryland

Central Maryland became the center of *industry* in the state. Mills made the farmers' grain into flour. Textile mills made cloth for clothing and sails. Local mines produced iron. Iron was made into nails and other products. Many people found jobs in these industries.

Joseph Ellicott and his brothers built mills by the falls along the Patapsco River. Some mill towns had housing for the workers, stores where they could buy what they needed, and churches where they could worship.

Central Maryland had two main cities—Annapolis and Baltimore. Annapolis had fine shops, many lawyers and professional people, and government workers. A lot of people, including free blacks and slaves, worked at skilled crafts, businesses, and in the ports. Annapolis had good music and theater for the people to enjoy.

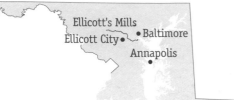

Ellicott's Mills was built along the Pataptsco River.

The Maryland Adventure

The Waterwheel

▼ Drawing by Jon Burton

Mills ran on waterpower. In this gristmill, water from a river or waterfall made a large wheel go around and around. As the wheel turned, it moved levers that turned a millstone. As the millstone turned, it ground wheat into flour. The flour was then packaged and taken to market.

Can you see why there were so many jobs in Baltimore's shipping industry?

Baltimore

Baltimore was the state's business center. Merchants shipped grain to other states and to the West Indies. New banks opened. Some merchants and bankers became very wealthy. The work of these men helped Baltimore grow.

Ship builders, captains, and sailors lived near the water. Workers hauled goods to and from the port. They loaded and unloaded the ships. They built roads, houses, warehouses, and wagons. Skilled craftspeople made more of the things people needed to live.

Some women worked to earn money. They ran boarding houses where newcomers to the city could live. Some did laundry. Some did sewing. Everyday jobs like cooking and cleaning took much longer than they do today, but they were just as necessary as they are today.

Many free black people came to Baltimore. There were lots of jobs there. Slaves escaped to Baltimore because they could disappear in the crowds. People from European countries and other states also came to Baltimore. It was the most *diverse* place in Maryland.

The Maryland Adventure

THE WAR OF 1812

The United States had won its independence from England, but there were still troubles between the two countries. They still argued over land and trading rights. Both sides got more and more angry. Soon the U.S. was fighting another war with England.

This time, Maryland was a center of *military* action. Important battles took place here, both on land and on the Chesapeake Bay. In the spring of 1813, British ships sailed up the Chesapeake Bay. They bombed the town of St. Michaels and burned Havre de Grace.

Marylanders knew all about the bay and our many rivers. Captain Thomas Boyle captured at least thirty British ships. He was a local hero.

The Battle of Bladensburg and the Burning of Washington

The British sailed up the Patuxent River and landed near Upper Marlboro. They sent soldiers marching towards Washington, D.C.

Joshua Barney and his navy men stood their ground at Bladensburg, but the Americans could not hold back the British. They pushed on to the capital. They set fire to the White House, the Capitol, and the naval yard. Many government officers fled from the city. Then the British headed toward Baltimore.

One of Maryland's most famous privateers was Joshua Barney.

British troops burned parts of Washington, D.C.

Bombs flew over Fort McHenry.

General Samuel Smith was the hero of the Battle of Baltimore.

The Battle of Baltimore

The Battle of Baltimore was a turning point in the war. The Americans won, but it was not an easy victory.

General Samuel Smith was in charge of defending the city. His strict training made the soldiers ready for battle. He put sixty large cannons at Fort McHenry at the mouth of Baltimore Harbor. Smith placed lookouts and warships along the route from North Point to the city.

In 1814, General Smith ordered all men who were not in the army, including free blacks and slaves, to report to Hampstead Hill to build forts. Baltimore's women made food for the workers. They helped nurse the wounded. They were not paid. They helped because they wanted to defend their city. Everyone joined in the effort to save Baltimore.

Smith had 15,000 men ready to meet the enemy when they landed at North Point. The British started to march towards the city. At the same time, the British navy moved ships around Fort McHenry. They began to attack the fort.

The Maryland soldiers forced the British to **retreat** at the Battle of Hampstead Hill. The Americans held Fort McHenry through a day and night of British bombing. The Americans had won, and the British left Baltimore.

After American troops won a second major battle in New York, the British decided that they were ready for peace. The War of 1812 was over and Marylanders could return to their normal lives.

The Maryland Adventure

The Star-Spangled Banner

The commander at Fort McHenry wanted a flag to mark his fort. He wanted it to be huge, so the enemy could see it from far away. A group of army officers chose Mary Pickersgill to make the flag.

Mary already knew how to make flags. She had made them for ships. She agreed to make a United States flag for the fort. Mary, her mother, and her thirteen-year-old daughter measured, cut, and sewed fifteen stars and stripes. But there was not enough room in their home to sew them all together. They used the floor of a nearby brewery to sew the flag each evening by candlelight. The women were paid about $400 for their work.

Francis Scott Key was on board a ship in Baltimore Harbor while the British were bombing Fort McHenry. As night came, the bombs continued to fall. When daylight returned, Key saw that the large American flag was still flying over the fort. He knew that we had defended our fort successfully. To celebrate he wrote a poem. It became our national *anthem*. It is called "The Star-Spangled Banner."

Mary Pickersgill of Baltimore worked with her mother and daughter to make the large flag that flew over Fort McHenry. The flag inspired Francis Scott Key to write "The Star-Spangled Banner."

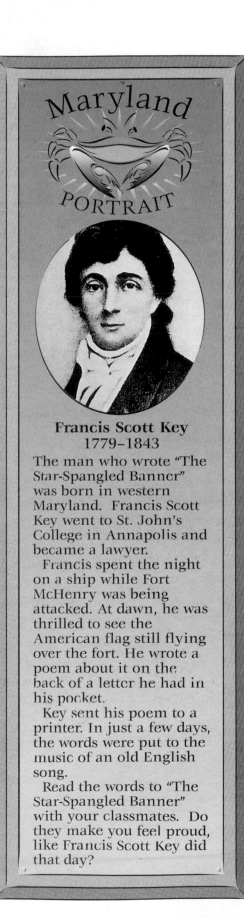

Maryland PORTRAIT

**Francis Scott Key
1779–1843**

The man who wrote "The Star-Spangled Banner" was born in western Maryland. Francis Scott Key went to St. John's College in Annapolis and became a lawyer.

Francis spent the night on a ship while Fort McHenry was being attacked. At dawn, he was thrilled to see the American flag still flying over the fort. He wrote a poem about it on the back of a letter he had in his pocket.

Key sent his poem to a printer. In just a few days, the words were put to the music of an old English song.

Read the words to "The Star-Spangled Banner" with your classmates. Do they make you feel proud, like Francis Scott Key did that day?

The Waterloo Inn was a stagecoach stop between Washington and Baltimore. Passengers stopped there to eat and rest during the long journey. It took five hours to go by coach from Washington to Baltimore. How long does this drive take today?

CHANGES IN TRANSPORTATION

With the return of peace, Marylanders could focus on building their state. They wanted to build new roads, canals, railroads, and buildings.

Building Better Roads

Maryland's public roads were very bad. They were made of dirt. In dry weather, dust flew everywhere. Wet weather meant that stagecoaches often got stuck in thick mud. Some roads had holes that were three feet deep.

To make the roads better, some companies built turnpikes, or roads with hard surfaces. The companies could charge a toll to everyone who traveled on the roads. Soon roads connected all of the major towns in Maryland.

The National Road

After the Revolution, families began to move into the Ohio River Valley. They raised cattle and grew grain. They wanted to sell their crops in eastern cities, but it was hard to move things all the way across the Appalachian Mountains.

To make things easier, the government built a road that went across several states. It was wide enough for wagons and stagecoaches. It was called the National Road.

The National Road started in Cumberland, Maryland. It connected towns in several states. Over time, the road stretched farther west. Soon it reached Illinois.

Many people worked on building the road. They sweated all day, chopping down trees and digging paths through thick grass and over high ridges. It was hard work to cut through the mountain rocks. They worked until their muscles ached.

When the National Road opened, stagecoaches and wagons carried people and goods from the city and countryside. Farmers drove herds of cattle, sheep, and pigs along the road to market. Letters and newspapers from towns in the East were sent to people in the West. Families who had moved far away from home were glad to be able to read them.

The National Road was a little higher in the middle than along the sides. This allowed water and snow to drain off into the ditches on each side.

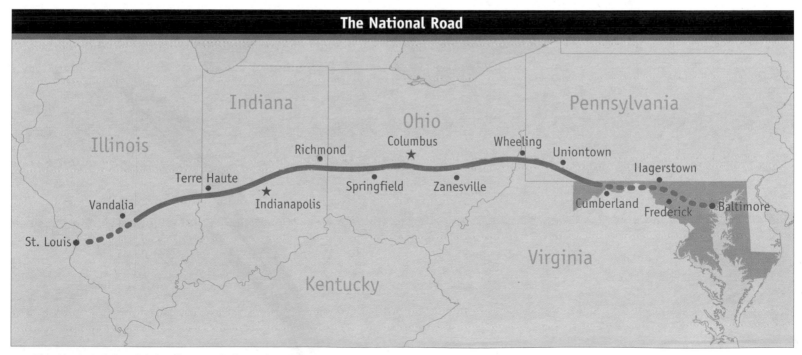

The National Road joined a road that already went from Baltimore to Cumberland. Goods brought from the West to Baltimore could then be shipped to other parts of the country and the world.

Canals

Canals were another way to connect places. It was easier to move heavy goods by water than across the land. But the rivers didn't always flow where the people wanted to go. The people built canals to connect one river to another. Then they had an all-water route. Maryland built two successful canals.

Projects like the C & O Canal were often paid for by selling lottery tickets.

• The Chesapeake and Ohio Canal connected Washington to western Maryland. It was nicknamed the C & O Canal.

• The Chesapeake and Delaware Canal linked the Delaware Bay and the Chesapeake Bay. Ships still use this canal today.

A special kind of boat worked best on the canals. Canal boats had flat bottoms and were very long. They did not have engines. Mules pulled them along with heavy ropes. The mules walked along a towpath beside the canal.

Often an entire family lived on a canal boat. They made their living hauling goods back and forth along the canal. The canal boat had a small cabin in the back with bunk beds. The mules slept in a stable in the front of the boat.

Many young boys wanted the job of driving the mules along the path.

This canal boat had a striped shade to keep the hot sun off the passengers. Can you see the mule on the towpath?

Railroads

On the same day workers began building the C & O Canal, other workers began building the Baltimore and Ohio Railroad. Railroads were very new at the time. The B & O was the first railroad in the United States.

The men worked quickly. By 1830, the tracks ran from Baltimore to Ellicott's Mills. The next year, they went on to Frederick. Finally the tracks reached Cumberland.

Steam trains could carry heavy coal from Cumberland to the rest of Maryland. This meant that places that did not have their own supply of coal could bring in fuel from other places. For example, the town of Laurel built mills and a machine shop. These industries made jobs for hundreds of people.

Many people did not think that the trains would work. When a horse beat the engine Tom Thumb in a race, they were sure that the new invention would soon disappear.

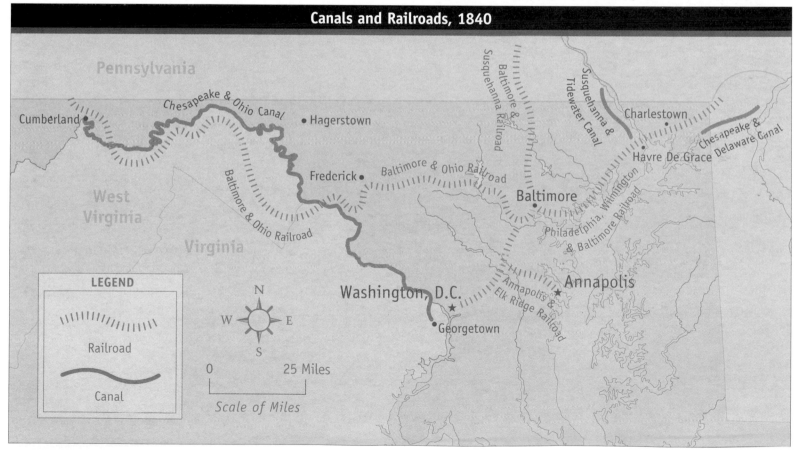

Look at the new routes the canals and railroads made. Find the Chesapeake and Delaware Canal. What other railroads besides the B & O do you see?

Most of the work building the canals was done by immigrants. Horses helped haul away the dirt the men dug out of the canal bed. From what is shown in this picture, can you list three jobs the workers had to do?

IMMIGRANT WORKERS

There were not enough American workers to build all the new roads, canals, and railroads. So companies spread the word to European countries that there were jobs in America. Many people left their homes and families to come to the United States. They called it the "land of opportunity."

Immigrants from Europe came on ships to Baltimore and Annapolis. These workers, farmers, and craftsmen helped build our state and our nation. Often they had very difficult lives.

Irish Immigrants

In Ireland, many families were poor. (Ireland belonged to England, just as the American colonies had.) Irish people survived on potatoes, a crop that grew well there. But one year a disease hit the potato plants. The potatoes rotted.

People in Ireland were starving. Many left Ireland to come to the United States. Some came to Maryland.

Many of the Irish immigrants had been too poor to go to school in Ireland. When they arrived in America, they had to take jobs that did not require an education. Irish men helped build the roads, canals, and railroads that were so important to our young nation.

Irish women cleaned and did laundry for other families. Children helped the adults. They gave their pennies to the family to buy food or pay rent.

German Immigrants

Many immigrants from Germany had better lives. Some were educated. Some worked in skilled trades making furniture or glass. Some had been able to save money back home. They used their savings to start a business or buy a farm.

Other Germans were very poor. They had no savings. They sold their labor like the indentured servants who came during colonial times.

The story of the ship *Juffrow Johanna* shows the hard life some of these people had to face:

A ship of . . . 300 German men, women and children has arrived off Annapolis. . . . where she is [blocked] by ice. These people have been fifteen weeks on board and are short of [food and water]. . . . Their bedding, having become filthy, was thrown overboard. They are now actually [dying] from the cold and want of [food and water].

—*The Baltimore American*

For six weeks, the ship was stranded. Soon the captain put an advertisement in the newspaper. He offered ". . . farmers and mechanics of all sorts, and several fine young boys and girls . . ." They would work without pay until their masters felt they had gotten their money's worth.

Helping Each Other

Many Marylanders noticed the problems of the new immigrants. They formed groups to help the newcomers find homes and jobs. They worked to protect their rights.

*Gruber's German Almanac was printed in Hagerstown and read by people who spoke German. An **almanac** is a book that gives lots of good information, such as when to plant crops, the phases of the moon, and dates of holidays. At first, Gruber wrote the almanac in German. Later he wrote it in English because the children and grandchildren of the early German settlers had learned to speak and read English.*

NEW RIGHTS AND FREEDOMS

Do you remember what the Declaration of Independence said? It said that all men were created equal. But we know that all people were not treated equally in their daily lives.

Many men, women, and children were slaves, with almost no rights. Immigrants were often treated terribly and had to work for very low pay. Women still could not vote or own land.

But things were changing for the better. More African Americans had become free. More people did have the right to vote. Men who did not own land won the right to vote. Jewish men, who were helping to build Maryland, won the right to vote and hold public office.

People were free to choose their own religion. No one religion had special privileges anymore. The early English settlers were Catholic or Protestant. Africans brought their own religions with them. Many later became Christians. The Scotch-Irish were Presbyterians. German immigrants brought the Lutheran religion with them. They worshipped and sang in German.

Quakers, who first came from England, wanted to change society. They freed their slaves and protested against slavery. Many Quakers were also against war. They believed there were other ways of solving problems.

Most of the Jews in Baltimore had come from Germany. They started the Baltimore Hebrew Congregation. They invited a rabbi from Germany, Abraham Rice, to lead the *congregation*.

Maryland was also an important center for the Methodist Church. Methodist leaders were especially concerned with working people. They made a special effort to reach out to slaves and free blacks. Francis Asbury, the first Methodist bishop in America, was *ordained* in Maryland.

John Carroll became the first Roman Catholic bishop in America.

Rabbi Abraham Rice led Jews in Baltimore.

Bethel African Methodist Episcopal Church was one of the first in the nation.

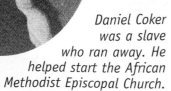

Daniel Coker was a slave who ran away. He helped start the African Methodist Episcopal Church.

EDUCATION

Most boys and girls did not get the chance to go to school 200 years ago. Many children worked on farms, in mills, or at jobs in the cities. They did not have the time to go to school. Sometimes farm children went to school for just a few months during the winter when they did not have to help with the crops.

Books were very expensive then, and most families owned only a few. If a family could afford one book, they usually had a Bible. Children learned to read by reading the Bible. Families also kept records of births, marriages, and deaths in their Bibles.

Wealthy children had tutors who came to their homes. They had their own libraries. Some children went to private schools. A private school is a school that the students' parents have to pay for.

In 1826, a new law allowed cities and counties to open public schools. Public schools had no special fee. This was a beginning towards education for all. However, none of the public schools let in African American children.

Colleges and Universities

Two early Maryland colleges are still educating students today. Washington College, the first in Maryland, opened in Chestertown in 1782. Two years later, St. John's College opened in Annapolis.

The Medical College of Maryland opened in Baltimore in 1807 to train medical doctors. A dental school followed. These later became the University of Maryland.

St. John's College still educates students today.

Early Schools in Maryland

St. Joseph's School for Girls was started in Baltimore by Elizabeth Seton. She became a nun and wanted to teach girls. Long after she died, the Roman Catholic Church made her a *saint*. She was the first saint in the United States.

Elizabeth Seton

Watkins' Academy was started by William Watkins for African American students. His niece, Frances Watkins Harper, studied there until she was thirteen. Later, she became a teacher. She wrote poetry that is read by many people today.

Frances Watkins Harper

Using a Graph

Graphs and charts help us to see a lot of information in a simple way. Use the population graph to answer the questions.

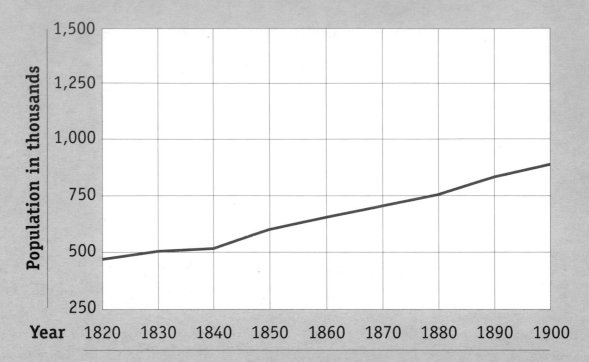

1. How many people lived in Maryland in 1830?

2. How many people lived in Maryland fifty years later?

3. Did Maryland have more or fewer people in 1900 than in 1850?

4. In what ten-year period did the population stay about the same?

The Atlantic was an early locomotive.

The Maryland Adventure

1. What crop did many farmers in southern Maryland grow?
2. What became the most important town on the Eastern Shore?
3. Who was the hero of the Battle of Baltimore?
4. Who wrote "The Star Spangled Banner"?
5. Why was the National Road built? Where did it begin?
6. How did canals make transportation easier?
7. What was the first railroad in the United States?
8. List two of the countries immigrants came from during this time.
9. List three religions in Maryland during this time.
10. Why did most boys and girls only go to school for part of the year?

Geography Tie-In

Look at the map below. Where in Maryland did major battles take place during the War of 1812? Which battle happened first? Which happened second and third? Use your finger to trace the routes the British may have used to reach those places.

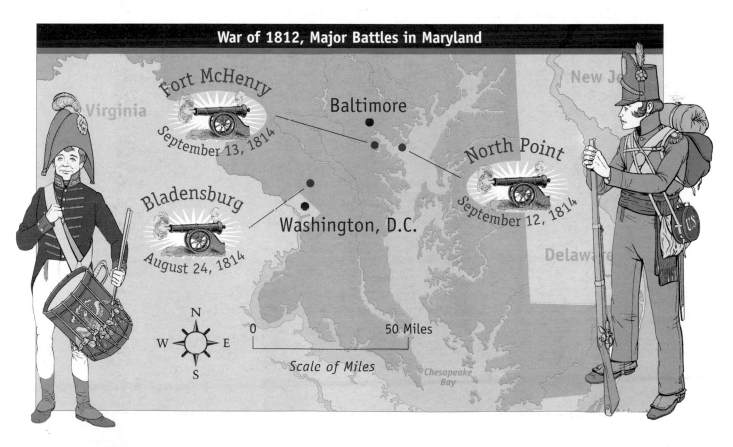

War of 1812, Major Battles in Maryland

Fort McHenry
September 13, 1814

Baltimore

North Point
September 12, 1814

Bladensburg
August 24, 1814

Washington, D.C.

Virginia

New Jersey

Delaware

Chesapeake Bay

0   50 Miles

Scale of Miles

N W E S

**THE TIME
1850–1870**

Two Marylands:
The Civil War

*During the Civil War, soldiers fought and fell
at Antietam National Battlefield.*
(Photo by Tom Till)

timeline of events

1850–1865
Some slaves escape to freedom on the Underground Railroad.

1860
Baltimore has the largest community of
free African Americans in the country.

1850

1855

TERMS TO UNDERSTAND
outlaw
overseer
rebellion
determined
emancipation
abolitionist
sccede
Confederacy
Union
border state
assassinate

1863
The Emancipation Proclamation
ends slavery in the South. A new
state constitution is passed, making
slavery illegal in Maryland.

1864
Lincoln is re-elected
as president.

1870
The Fifteenth Amendment gives African
Americans the right to vote.

1860

1865

1870

1862 Battle of Antietam

1861
Abraham Lincoln becomes president.
A group of southern states leaves the Union.
The Baltimore Riot

1865
April 14 Lincoln is shot.
He dies the next day.

1861–1865
The Civil War

107

A Nation Divided

BY THE MIDDLE OF THE 1800s, our state had grown and changed. So had our country. Different parts of the country grew in different ways.

In the North, industry and business became very important. People built new cities. Some cities grew very large.

The northern states *outlawed* slavery. Some people had small farms, but they could do most of the work themselves. Most of the powerful people worked in business.

In the South, farming was still the most important part of the economy. Cotton was the most important crop. Slaves did a lot of the hard work. Many of the powerful people owned large plantations. Cities in the South were smaller than cities in the North.

Because of all their differences, the North and the South wanted different things from the government. The North wanted it to help business and industry. The South wanted it to help agriculture.

The biggest issue between the two regions was slavery. More and more, people in the North criticized Southerners for owning slaves. Most Northerners said that slavery was wrong.

Many Southerners believed that they needed slaves to produce the cotton that brought wealth to the South. They saw nothing wrong with the system of slavery that had existed for hundreds of years.

A State Divided

Maryland sits right between the northern states and southern states.

Maryland was part North and part South. Northern and western Maryland were like

The North

The South

Old Home

▲ Drawing by Jon Burton

the North in many ways. Southern Maryland and the Eastern Shore were more like the South.

The national government let each state decide whether it would have slavery. States without slavery were called "free" states. States that allowed slavery were called "slave" states. Maryland was a slave state. However, there were many free blacks living in Maryland.

Many people in Maryland did business with both the North and the South. More than anything, they wanted to avoid a war. War would hurt their business.

SLAVERY

The Declaration of Independence said that "all men are created equal." But slaves were not considered equal to other people. They were thought of as property. Slavery was a terrible part of the history of Maryland and our whole nation.

Some of our great-great grandfathers and grandmothers were slaves. Some were slave owners. Some of our grandparents were not even in this country in the days of slavery. Today, we are neither slaves nor slave owners. But it is important for us to understand what slavery was like because it is a part of our history.

Roger B. Taney [TAW ney] of Maryland was in favor of slavery. He became Chief Justice of the U.S. Supreme Court.

W h a t   d o   y o u   t h i n k ?

- How have the good and bad actions of our ancestors affected us?
- How can we help heal the problems of the past?

Slaves at Work

Most slaves worked on plantations. Men, women and children over the age of six put seeds in the ground, took care of the plants, and harvested the crops. They worked twelve or fourteen hours a day in the hot sun or the rain.

Some slaves learned skilled crafts. They worked as carpenters, blacksmiths, and boot makers. In Maryland, some slaves worked in iron mines and in industries. A few worked in shops and offices. Some cooked and cleaned and took care of children in the master's house. Maryland slaves made many important contributions to the life of our state.

Maryland Governor Augustus Bradford was against slavery.

> "My brothers and sisters were bid off first . . . while my mother . . . held me by the hand. Then I was offered. My mother pushed through the crowd to the spot where [her master] was standing. She fell at his knees, [begging] him . . . to buy her baby as well as herself."
>
> —*Josiah Henson*
> *a Maryland slave*

Women worked in the fields from sunup to sundown. At night their backs ached from bending over all day.

Advertisements of slaves for sale were seen in newspapers all the time.

FOR SALE,
A young likely NEGRO,
About 18 years of age—a very good waiter, good
carriage driver, and a very good hostler; en-
quire of the Printer, at his offices in Bond-
Street, and No. 15, Baltimore-Street.
May 31.

Butter & Mackerel.
One Hundred Barrels best Boston Bay
MACKEREL,
of an excellent quality---superior to those gen
rally offered for sale at this season of the yea

Slave Families

Like all people, slave children had a mother and a father. Many had sisters and brothers, aunts and uncles, grandmothers and grandfathers. Often, family members lived near each other. But, at any time, an owner could sell a slave to someone who lived far away.

At slave auctions, where slaves were sold to the highest bidders, mothers were dragged from their children. Brothers and sisters were torn apart. Sometimes they never saw each other again. Even if everybody cried, it did no good.

Slaves were not allowed to control their own lives. They could only dream of going to college. In fact, they could not go to school at all. They could not even choose their own jobs.

Punishments

If a slave did something the owner did not like, the owner might whip or beat the slave. Sometimes an owner with a lot of slaves hired an **overseer** to make sure the slaves did their work. The overseer gave out punishments so the owner did not have to do this unpleasant job himself.

Most Marylanders did not like it when slave owners used cruel punishments. But, most of the time, no one stopped the slave owners.

What do you think**?**

Why is it important to remember the terrible, sad parts of history as well as the good parts?

Many Slaves Rebelled

It is no surprise that slaves did not like living under such cruel conditions. Many of them protested. Some slaves rose up in *rebellion* against their owners. Many more just ran away.

Some slaves did not want to risk the punishment they would get if they were caught planning a rebellion or trying to escape. Often they just decided not to work very hard. That was another way to rebel against slavery.

The overseer watched from his horse as slaves worked the young tobacco plants.

THE UNDERGROUND RAILROAD

Some free blacks and whites joined together to help slaves escape to the North. They set up a secret system called the Underground Railroad. The Underground Railroad was not really a railroad. It was a system of secret routes that slaves used to escape. It was not really underground, either. "Underground" just means that it was hidden from most people.

The people who helped the runaways were called "conductors." They hid slaves in their homes, barns, and churches as they moved north. These safe hiding places were called "stations." There were Underground Railroad stations all the way to Canada.

Many slaves traveled north on boats that sailed up the Chesapeake Bay. The bay was a route to freedom. Some ship captains were conductors on the Underground Railroad. Other slaves traveled without the help of conductors. They just "followed the North Star to freedom."

RAN AWAY!

FROM THE SUBSCRIBER. My Mulatto Boy, GEORGE. Said George is 5 feet 8 inches in height, brown curly Hair, dark coat. I will give $400 for him alive, and the same sum for satisfactory proof that he has been killed.

Vide ANTHONY & ELLIS' MAMMOTH "UNCLE TOM'S CABIN."

WM. HARRIS.

Some masters hunted down their runaway slaves. The masters offered a reward for their capture. If caught, the slaves were whipped, tortured, and sometimes killed.

Harriet Tubman

One of the most famous conductors was Harriet Tubman. She was born a slave on a plantation in Dorchester County. As a young girl, Harriet was hired out to do work on different farms.

When Harriet was twenty-four years old she married John Tubman, a free black man. Five years later she escaped to the North. She was free!

Harriet didn't stop with her own freedom. She risked her life again and again by returning to the South to help other slaves escape. Over many years, she led about 300 slaves to freedom. Two of them were her own parents.

Harriet Tubman's home in New York was a station on the Underground Railroad. When war broke out between the North and South, she worked as a spy for the North. This brave woman showed that one person can make a difference in many people's lives.

In this picture, Harriet Tubman works on a "signal quilt." If the quilt was hanging on a clothesline, the slaves knew it was safe to come to that house.

FREE BLACKS

Across Maryland, many African Americans were free. In cities such as Baltimore and Annapolis, and in some small towns, they built churches and schools.

Sandy Springs was a Quaker settlement. The Quaker families had freed their slaves. The former slaves built a free community there.

Some free African Americans opened businesses. A few were professionals, such as teachers and ministers. Many were laborers who worked hard to get enough money to buy food and pay rent.

In rural areas, most free blacks were farmers. Some were able to buy land of their own. Others worked for pay on someone else's land. Some were craftspeople who sold the things they made.

As the years passed, more and more African Americans in Maryland were free. By 1860, just before the Civil War began, about one half were free. Baltimore had the largest free African American community in the whole country.

"I looked at my hands to see if I was the same person now I was free. There was such a glory through the trees and over the hills, and I felt like I was in heaven."

—Harriet Tubman

Frederick Douglass

Frederick Douglass was born in Tuckahoe. He was a slave because his mother was a slave. When Frederick was seven, he was sent to live on another plantation. His mother walked the twelve miles to see him as often as she could. Usually she could do this only on Sundays.

After his mother died, young Frederick was sent to Baltimore to live with the Auld family. His job was to help care for their young son and to do chores around the house.

As a teenager, Frederick Douglass worked in a shipyard. One day some white workers beat him up. Douglass could not have his attackers arrested. They could never be tried for the crime because African Americans were not allowed to testify in court.

Mrs. Auld was teaching her son to read and write. She began to teach Frederick at the same time. Then Mr. Auld stopped the lessons. It was not against the law for slaves in Maryland to learn to read and write, but many slave owners did not like the idea. They knew that if slaves could read and write it would be easier for them to escape or plan rebellions.

Frederick was **determined** to learn. He figured out a way to do this. When he was with friends on the street, he showed them the letters that he knew. He bet them that they could not write as many letters as he could. Soon they wrote other letters. That is how Frederick Douglass learned the whole alphabet. Soon he could read everything.

In the city, Frederick earned money doing odd jobs. With his first cash, he bought a book. He believed education was the way to freedom.

When Frederick was twenty, he escaped and went north. He joined men and women who were working very hard to end slavery. He began an anti-slavery newspaper. He called his newspaper *The North Star*.

"Education . . . means *emancipation*; it means light and liberty."
—*Frederick Douglass*

Slaves rebelled at Harpers Ferry, just across the Potomac River from Maryland.

Elisha Tyson, a Quaker, was a famous abolitionist from Maryland.

ABOLITIONISTS

People across the country who worked to end slavery were called *abolitionists*. They were male and female, black and white, young and old. They shared a belief that slavery was wrong.

Frederick Douglass was an important abolitionist. He traveled across the nation giving speeches about the awful lives that slaves were forced to live. Harriet Tubman also spoke to crowds about her life as a slave. Their speeches convinced many people that slavery had to end.

The famous writer Harriet Beecher Stowe wrote a story about slavery. Her book is called *Uncle Tom's Cabin*. She based the most important character on a Maryland slave, Josiah Henson. His stories made the suffering of slaves real to her. Her book reached many readers and turned them against slavery.

Many Quakers were abolitionists. They said that all people are equal in the eyes of God. Quakers were conductors on the Underground Railroad. They taught African American students to read and write. Benjamin Lundy was a Quaker from Baltimore. He printed the country's first anti-slavery newspaper.

Another white abolitionist, John Brown, led a rebellion against slavery. He and a group of men took guns from an army storehouse near Harpers Ferry, Virginia. Brown planned to give the guns to slaves, who could then fight for their own freedom. The Maryland militia helped capture John Brown and the others. Brown was hanged for treason.

The Maryland Adventure

THINGS GET WORSE BETWEEN THE NORTH AND SOUTH

Americans argued about the issues that divided the North and South. Congressmen and senators in Washington disagreed on everything from taxes to slavery.

Northerners said that people from the South were bad people because they owned slaves. Southerners said that northern industries made cloth from cotton grown by slaves. So, they said, the Northerners had no right to criticize.

Tempers grew hot. The more the abolitionists attacked slavery, the more determined the slave owners became. They said they didn't want Northerners telling them what to do.

Abraham Lincoln

Abraham Lincoln

The United States held an election for a new president in 1860. Slavery was the big issue that everyone talked about. Four men were candidates. Abraham Lincoln, a lawyer from Illinois, was the winner.

Abraham Lincoln was against slavery. Most people in the South believed that Lincoln would abolish slavery. They believed that he would hurt the South. They were really angry that Lincoln had won.

The South Secedes

Across the South, people decided that they did not want to be a part of this country any longer. One by one, the southern states *seceded* from the United States.

The southern states formed their own government. They called themselves the Confederate States of America, or the *Confederacy*.

When the Confederate states seceded, our country was split in two. The northern states were called the *Union*. There were four slave states that did not leave the Union. Maryland was one of them. These four states were called *border states*.

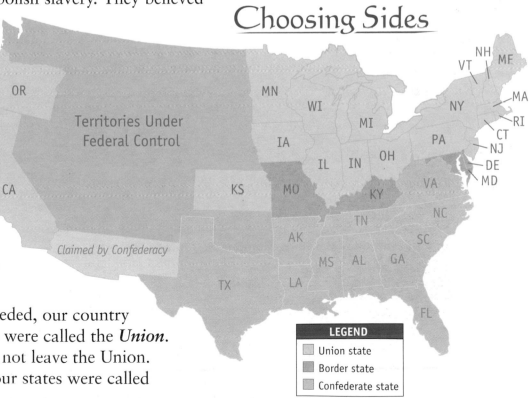

Choosing Sides

Territories Under Federal Control

Claimed by Confederacy

LEGEND
Union state
Border state
Confederate state

War Begins

President Lincoln said that states could not secede. He said that Americans would not be allowed to break up their country.

The Confederacy wanted to be on its own. Its men were armed and ready to fight. Soon, a civil war (a war between people in the same country) began.

THE CIVIL WAR IN MARYLAND

Because of Maryland's location, there was a lot of fighting in our state. Northern troops had to go through Maryland to get to the South. Southern troops came into Maryland trying to drive the Union soldiers back up north.

Many Marylanders fought in the Civil War. Most fought for the Union. Some fought for the Confederacy. Sometimes families were divided. From time to time, brothers fought against each other.

What do you think**?**

Would you want to live in a country where people went to war if they did not like the results of an election? Why or why not?

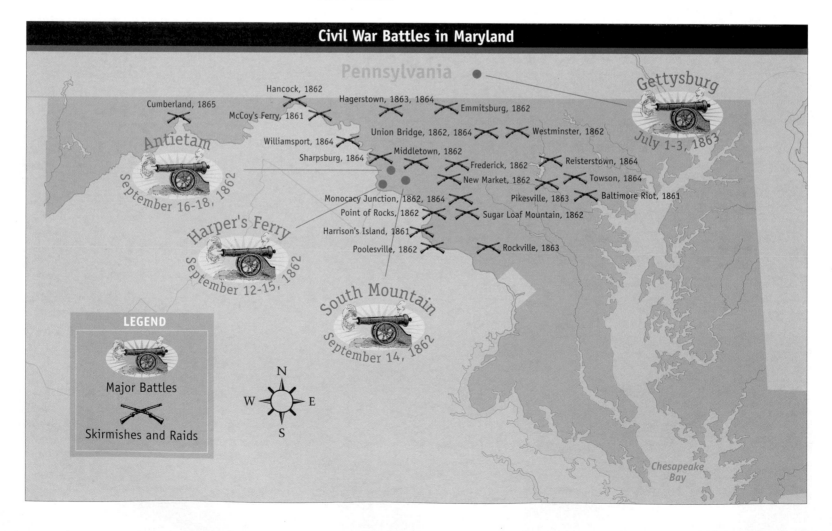

Civil War Battles in Maryland

Pennsylvania

Gettysburg
July 1-3, 1863

Cumberland, 1865

Hancock, 1862

Hagerstown, 1863, 1864

Emmitsburg, 1862

McCoy's Ferry, 1861

Union Bridge, 1862, 1864

Westminster, 1862

Antietam
September 16-18, 1862

Williamsport, 1864

Sharpsburg, 1864

Middletown, 1862

Frederick, 1862

Reisterstown, 1864

New Market, 1862

Towson, 1864

Monocacy Junction, 1862, 1864

Pikesville, 1863

Baltimore Riot, 1861

Point of Rocks, 1862

Sugar Loaf Mountain, 1862

Harper's Ferry
September 12-15, 1862

Harrison's Island, 1861

Poolesville, 1862

Rockville, 1863

South Mountain
September 14, 1862

LEGEND

Major Battles

Skirmishes and Raids

N
W E
S

Chesapeake Bay

The Baltimore Riot

Union soldiers from Massachusetts marched south to defend the nation's capital. They had to pass through Baltimore on their way. A few Marylanders did not want Union troops to march through their state. They attacked the troops. Before the street fighting ended, sixteen people were killed. These were the first deaths of the Civil War.

After the riot, the Union army stayed in Baltimore to make sure there was no more trouble. It was important for the Union to control the land next to Washington, D.C.

Union soldiers were attacked as they passed through Baltimore.

Union troops occupied Federal Hill in Baltimore. They stayed to make sure Baltimore remained loyal to the Union.

The Battle of Antietam

One of the most terrible battles of the Civil War took place in Maryland. Soldiers from the North and South fought in a field south of Hagerstown, near Antietam Creek. Before the day was over, 23,000 soldiers lay dead or wounded. It was the bloodiest one-day battle of the whole war.

Neither side really won the Battle of Antietam. Confederate General Robert E. Lee's army retreated into Virginia. The Northerners did not follow them.

Soldiers lay dead in front of the Dunker Church. Anyone who saw Antietam knew the cost of war.

Every building around Antietam and Sharpsburg sheltered wounded soldiers. President Lincoln visited the site of this awful massacre.

The Battle of Gettysburg

The next year, the Confederate army returned to western Maryland. This time they marched through Maryland into southern Pennsylvania. Union troops met them at a town called Gettysburg. There the Union won a clear victory. It was the turning point of the Civil War.

The Maryland Adventure

Barbara Fritchie

Barbara Fritchie waves her Union flag.

Barbara Fritchie had lived in Frederick for ninety-three years. When she heard that Union troops were marching through her town, she waved the Union flag out her window.

The troops turned out to be Confederate soldiers. Barbara continued to wave her flag to show her loyalty to the Union. A Confederate soldier saw this and warned her to take her flag inside. She kept waving the flag. Then the soldier asked his leader for permission to shoot Barbara Fritchie.

An American poet, John Greenleaf Whittier, wrote a poem about Barbara Fritchie. This is how he says the story ended:

'Shoot if you must, this old gray head,
But spare your country's flag,' she said.
A shade of sadness, a blush of shame,
Over the face of the leader came.
The nobler nature within him stirred
To life at that woman's deed and word,
'Who touches a hair of yon gray head
Dies like a dog! March on!' he said.

A Soldier's Life

Many young men had joined the army thinking the war would be exciting and short. They dreamed of being brave heroes. But usually the war was not like that. Soldiers spent most days sitting in camp, waiting for a battle. When the battles came, they were horrible. Men were shot and killed. Some lost arms or legs.

Often the armies were not able to give soldiers the things they needed to live. Sometimes they did not have shoes. Sometimes soldiers ran out of food. If this happened, the soldiers often raided homes and farms to steal what they needed.

Diseases killed a lot of soldiers. The water supply was not always clean. Some army camps did not have sanitary facilities. Human waste lay all around. Men got sick and died.

Not all soldiers were men. Boys as young as thirteen left home for adventure or to escape bad conditions. Sometimes the boys were shot in battle. Other boys were drummers or buglers.

Sergeant Major Christian Fleetwood was awarded the Congressional Medal of Honor for bravery in battle.

Women and the War Effort

Women volunteered to nurse the wounded. They made clothes and bandages for the soldiers.

Some women served as spies. Harriet Tubman worked as a spy for the Union army. Another Maryland woman, Anna Ella Carroll, wrote battle plans that she sent to President Lincoln. Her plans showed a way to split the Confederacy into two parts so it could be attacked more easily. A few women even dressed up as men and joined the army.

The Emancipation Proclamation

Finally, President Lincoln decided that slavery must be abolished. In the middle of the war, he issued the Emancipation Proclamation. It said that all slaves in the Confederacy would be free.

Because Maryland was not in the Confederacy, the Emancipation Proclamation did not end slavery here. But Marylanders wrote a new constitution that made slavery illegal in our state.

PEACE AND FREEDOM

After four long years, the war finally ended. Confederate General Robert E. Lee surrendered to Union General Ulysses S. Grant. Everyone could finally go home.

The Civil War brought an end to slavery in the United States. Across the country men, women, and children became forever free. Also, the war had shown everyone that Americans could not split their country in two.

But not all of the results of the war were good. Families had lost fathers, brothers, and sons. Many homes and farms, especially in the South, had been destroyed. It was hard to put things back together after such great destruction.

Former slaves had another problem. In Maryland and across the South, many people left their homes in search of a new life. They had to find work. They had to provide their own food and shelter. They were still very poor. Freedom did not mean the end of everyone's problems.

The war did not bring an end to bad feelings between the North and the South. It would take many years for people on both sides to forgive each other.

Clara Barton traveled through Maryland and Virginia with wagons full of medicine, bandages, and food. After the war was over, she helped locate missing soldiers. She started the American Red Cross.

President Lincoln Is Assassinated

Right after the war ended, President Lincoln was killed. The president was watching a play when he was *assassinated* by a Marylander named John Wilkes Booth. Booth blamed Lincoln for starting the Civil War.

After the shooting, Booth ran out of the theater. He rode on horseback to Charles County. He crossed the Potomac River into Virginia. There Booth and another man were trapped in a barn. Officials set the barn on fire to force the two to come out. Booth refused. He died in the blaze.

Several people who had helped Booth plan the shooting were hanged. But their death could not bring back President Lincoln.

As Lincoln watched a play at Ford's Theater in Washington, John Wilkes Booth shot him in the head.

Maryland after the War

African Americans in Maryland celebrated the end of slavery. But some white Marylanders did not want to treat African Americans as equals.

Even though slavery was over, laws discriminated against black people. They were not allowed to vote. Public schools did not allow black children to attend. It was hard for African Americans to get good jobs.

The Freedman's Bureau, a government agency, did help former slaves. The bureau built schools and gave food, shelter, and medical care to people who were in need.

African Americans helped themselves, too. They opened schools, often in church buildings. People with homes took in the homeless. Others fed the hungry until they could find work. It was a very difficult time.

Governor Thomas Swann took the Union's side. After the war, he felt it was best not to punish the Maryland men and women who had favored the Confederacy.

Voting Rights

Across the country, African Americans said they should be allowed to vote. Some whites agreed. When the Fifteenth Amendment to the U.S. Constitution became law, five years after the Civil War ended, African Americans gained the right to vote. Of course, only men could vote. No women were allowed to vote.

Cause and Effect

Whenever we do something there is an effect, or result. For example, when we enter a dark room and flip on the light switch, the room is filled with light. This is called cause and effect. The cause is flipping on the light switch. The effect is that the room is filled with light. Life is filled with cause-and-effect relationships. Events in history also have causes and effects.

CAUSE: Something that happened first and caused something else to happen

EFFECT: What happened as a result of the cause

Look at each pair of sentences below. On a separate piece of paper, write **"C"** for the cause and **"E"** for the effect.

EXAMPLE:

<u>C</u>   Abraham Lincoln issued the Emancipation Proclamation.

<u>E</u>   Slaves were freed.

1. _____ Farmers in the South planted huge crops of cotton and tobacco.

   _____ They needed lots of field workers.

2. _____ Some slaves made it to freedom.

   _____ Brave people risked their lives to escape from slavery.

3. _____ A slave girl was punished by the master.

   _____ A slave girl was caught learning to read.

4. _____ Abraham Lincoln loved to read books and newspapers.

   _____ Lincoln could talk about many different subjects.

5. _____ The southern states left the Union.

   _____ Lincoln was elected president.

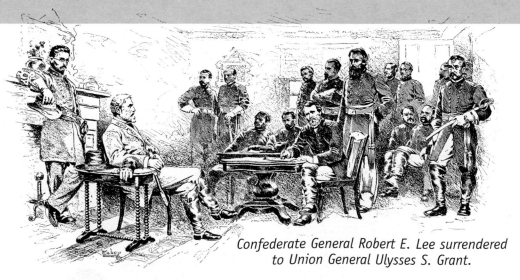

Confederate General Robert E. Lee surrendered to Union General Ulysses S. Grant.

The Maryland Adventure

1. How were the North and South different?

2. Was Maryland a free state or a slave state?

3. What was the Underground Railroad?

4. Name a famous conductor on the Underground Railroad who came from Maryland.

5. Name a famous abolitionist from Maryland who was born a slave.

6. Who was president of the United States during the Civil War?

7. After Lincoln became president, the southern states left the Union. What did they call themselves?

8. Where were the first people killed in the Civil War?

9. Where did the bloodiest one-day battle of the Civil War take place?

10. How did women help in the war?

11. What caused the death of President Abraham Lincoln?

12. Which amendment to the U.S. Constitution gave African Americans the right to vote?

Geography Tie-In

What facts of geography made Maryland so important during the Civil War?

When African Americans won the right to vote, there were big celebrations. In Baltimore, men who had fought in the Civil War marched in a parade.

This wagon picked up children to take them to school in Damascus. How is it different from your school bus today?

1870
African Americans win
the right to vote.

1890
Harry Cummings is the first black
man on the Baltimore City Council.

timeline of events   1870   1880

1876
Alexander Graham Bell
invents the telephone.

1880–1910
Waves of immigrants come to Maryland.

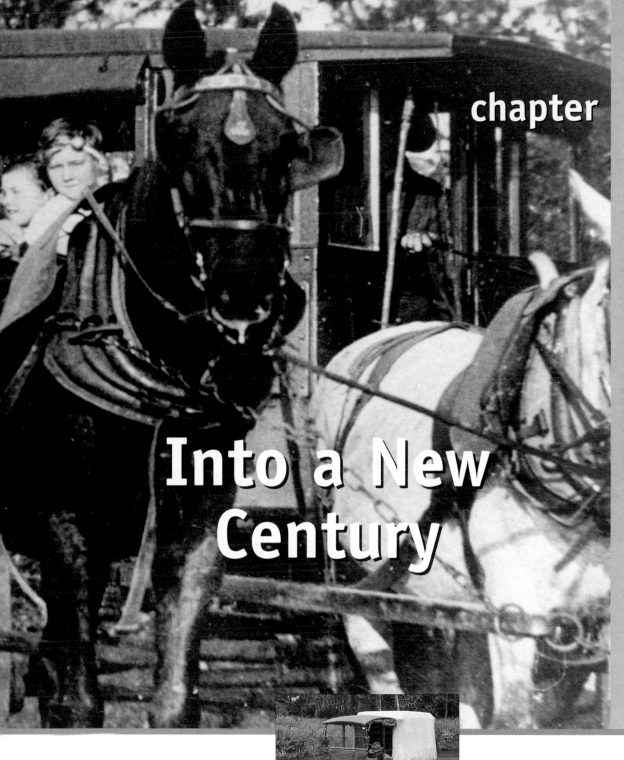

chapter

7

TERMS TO UNDERSTAND
century
migrant
Industrial Revolution
mass production
ghetto
kerosene
generator
reliable
suburb
segregate
Progressive
politics
union
philanthropist

Into a New Century

1893
The first gasoline-powered automobiles are invented.

1895
Radio is invented.

1900

1910

1914-1918
World War I
The U.S. enters the war in 1917.

1920

1920
Women win the right to vote.

A New America

WE HAVE SEEN HOW MARYLAND changed during the 1800s. It would change even more during the 1900s. As the new *century* began, immigrants poured into the state. Cities grew. New industries were started. Marylanders tried to put the Civil War behind them. They worked hard to build a new America.

A century is 100 years.

Maryland's natural resources provided the materials that made our industries successful. Our soil, water, and minerals gave the people many ways of making a living.

On the Farm

Farm families in the late 1800s grew grains, vegetables, and fruits. They produced meat and dairy products.

People who owned large farms hired workers to help with the harvest. They hired *migrant* workers who moved from farm to farm as different crops became ripe.

Migrant families started work as early as 4:30 in the morning. Many were immigrants from other countries. Some of these people did the work that slaves had done before the Civil War.

Laura Petty's family were migrant workers. She earned two cents for each box of berries she picked.

This boy was a member of the Laytonsville Pig Club. Boys in the club learned to take care of farm animals.

The Maryland Adventure

On the Water

Workers harvested oysters and fish from the Chesapeake Bay and nearby rivers. Companies sold the oysters and fish in Maryland and other states. John Crisfield built a railroad to move the seafood to Philadelphia and New York. The town of Crisfield is named after him.

Crisfield

Miners often took a canary underground with them. They knew that if the canary died, they had to get out fast because the bad air would soon kill them, too.

In the Mines

Western Maryland had valuable minerals such as coal and iron. Families heated their homes with coal. Coal was also burned to make the steam engines work on ships and trains.

Coal is found underground. To get to it, men and boys had to go into deep mines. They dug out the coal by hand. It was a very dangerous job. At any time, the ground above might collapse. It was also unhealthy work because the dust from coal caused lung disease.

Coal was shipped to industrial plants across the state. The dangerous work of the miners provided fuel for big industries.

Iron, steel, copper, and tin were other important minerals. Maryland's largest steel plant was at Sparrows Point. The workers used steel to make parts for ships and railroad tracks. Countries around the world bought tracks that were made in Maryland.

In the Factories

Machines had been invented that could make things faster than people could by hand. This was the beginning of the *Industrial Revolution*.

In Maryland, Baltimore led the Industrial Revolution. Cities like Cumberland, Hagerstown, Frederick, and Salisbury joined in. People in towns all across Maryland built small industries. People left the farms to work in the factories.

Men, women, and children worked in factories that processed food. They turned grain into flour. They canned fruits and vegetables. They canned oysters from the Chesapeake Bay.

Marylanders manufactured clothing, especially men's clothing. Local factories also made hats. Soon people were going to stores to buy clothes that had been made in factories, just like most of us do today.

So much production made our country rich and strong. It made many goods available at a low price. But there were problems, too. Some people, including children, had to work long hours in unsafe factories. They were paid very low wages. Sometimes the machines injured workers. If a machine cut off a worker's hand, he was fired because he could no longer do his job. There was no insurance or unemployment pay.

These boys had a job canning oysters. Sharp metal made it a dangerous job.

These children worked in a place where vegetables were canned. Canning made it possible for people to eat summer vegetables all year long.

Mass Production

Companies started to make many goods at once, instead of one at a time. This is called *mass production*. How does mass production work? Let's use the example of a shirt.

If your mother sews a shirt at home, she cuts out the front, back, sleeves, and collar. One by one, she sews them together. Then she adds the buttons.

If shirts are mass produced, one person or machine cuts out all the fronts. Others cut the backs, sleeves, and collars. Someone sews all the backs and fronts together. Someone else sews on all the sleeves, and so on.

Mass production is fast! Because more shirts can be made in the same amount of time, each shirt can be sold for a lower price. Can you think of other examples of things that are mass produced?

Ships brought immigrants to Locust Point in Baltimore. How would you feel if you arrived in a country where you could not speak the language? What kinds of things would you worry about?

Five Reasons People Came to America

1. To escape poverty and poor living conditions
2. To enjoy the freedoms of democracy
3. To escape war
4. To be free to practice any religion
5. To join other family members who had come earlier

NEW IMMIGRANTS

With all of the new industries and growing cities, there were lots of jobs. People from other countries came to take these jobs. Some immigrants settled near farms and helped grow food.

People came to America from all over the world. They came from Japan, China, Mexico, the West Indies, and Canada. However, most of the immigrants who came to Maryland during this time were from Europe. They came from England, Ireland, and Germany, as they had for many years. New immigrants also came from southern and eastern Europe. They left their homes because of problems there. Like the earlier immigrants, most were very poor.

Many people left Italy because of droughts. There was very little rain. The crops would not grow, so there was not enough food to eat. Families left places like Poland and Greece because they felt that the government treated them unfairly.

Jews left Russia and Poland because they were not allowed to own land there. Often, Jews had been forced to live in a small area called a ***ghetto***. People had burned down their homes and synagogues. Many Jews came to the United States. They knew that our laws guaranteed freedom of religion.

Immigrants looked to America as a "land of opportunity." They hoped that they would find religious and political freedom here. They hoped that they could find good jobs, decent homes, and enough to eat. They hoped that life would be better for their children here than it was in the "old country."

Journey to America

"All of us poor people had to go down through a hole to the bottom of the ship. There was a big dark room down there with rows of wooden shelves all around where we were going to sleep—the Italian, the German, the Polish, the Swede, the French—every kind. . . . When the dinner bell rang we were all standing in line . . . waiting for soup and bread."

—Rosa Cristofero, Italy

"[There were] six of us kids . . . after two weeks and a bit seasick we unloaded . . . we got an eye exam. Some man came along. He gave us a box of food. We had a ticket on us because we could not speak English. In the box there was a banana. We didn't know how to eat it. We'd never seen bananas. Finally somebody realized that and showed us."

—Nicholas Gerros, Greece

Most immigrants brought only the few possessions that they could carry.

From the Old World to the New World

Norway
Sweden   Finland
Russia
Denmark
Canada
England   Poland
Ireland   Germany
China
Italy
Japan
United States
Greece

Mexico   West Indies

At the Hurst Dry Goods Company in Baltimore, **kerosene** was stored right next to cotton and grain. It could easily catch fire. The fire chief had complained about the dangerous conditions for many years.

One Sunday in 1904, fire broke out. High winds spread the flames all over the downtown area. No one died, but the fire destroyed over 1,500 buildings.

After the fire, Baltimore made new rules for building. People hoped that fire would never again destroy such a large area.

These workers are paving Main Street in Annapolis.

The Cities Grow

With all of the immigrants and farm workers coming to work in factories, the cities grew quickly. Towns became small cities. Everywhere people were building new industries, new streets, new stores, and new houses.

The port of Baltimore was full of big cargo ships. Steamships were taking the place of the old sailing ships. They brought immigrants to Maryland. They carried coal, steel, clothes, and food to other parts of the country and world. Isaac Myers, a leader in the African American community, opened a ship repair yard. He hired both black and white workers and paid them a fair wage.

INVENTIONS MAKE LIFE EASIER

Many things that we take for granted today did not exist 100 years ago. People did not have televisions or computers. Most did not have cars or telephones. If you could travel back in time—let's say to 1870—you would find that your life was very different.

Electricity

In 1870, if you wanted to cook or heat your house, you had to fill a stove with coal or wood, then light a fire. Today, you turn a knob to get gas or electric heat. In 1870, to get light, you filled a lamp with kerosene and trimmed the wick every day. Today, you flip a switch.

Electric *generators* were one of the most important new inventions. Generators are machines for making electricity. They changed the way people worked, played, and lived. Streets and homes were lit with electric lights for the first time. New machines that used electricity were invented. There were electric washing machines, irons, stoves, refrigerators, and vacuum cleaners. Streetcars no longer had to be pulled by horses. They could run on electric wires.

The Telephone

In 1870, if you wanted to talk to people across town, you had to write them a letter or go see them yourself.

Alexander Graham Bell's new invention—the telephone—made it easier for people to communicate. Soon Marylanders were making calls from town to town.

Over time, Bell's invention led to many other discoveries. Today, you can pick up the telephone and talk to people around the world. Your computer can use your phone line to send e-mail anywhere in the world.

A Sewer System

In 1870, most people went to a well or spring to get water. This took a lot of time. Sometimes the water was not clean. People's toilets drained straight into the ground. Sometimes human waste got into the well water that people drank. Children and adults died from terrible diseases.

Around 1900, Baltimore began to pump water from the Gunpowder River. This brought cleaner drinking water. People who could afford it had water pumped directly into their houses. Then they could just turn on the faucet to get water.

Baltimore built a sewer system to collect the waste water. The sewers carried the dirty water to a new treatment plant where it was cleaned. Soon smaller cities were building their own sewer systems.

Women used hand-powered washing machines. Today we use electric washing machines.

People took tours of the new sewers before they were put in use. Baltimore's sewer system was a model for the country.

Into a New Century

People often made fun of the early cars. When they saw a car in trouble, they yelled, "Get a horse!"

Trolleys shared the street with a few automobiles in the Hagerstown public square.

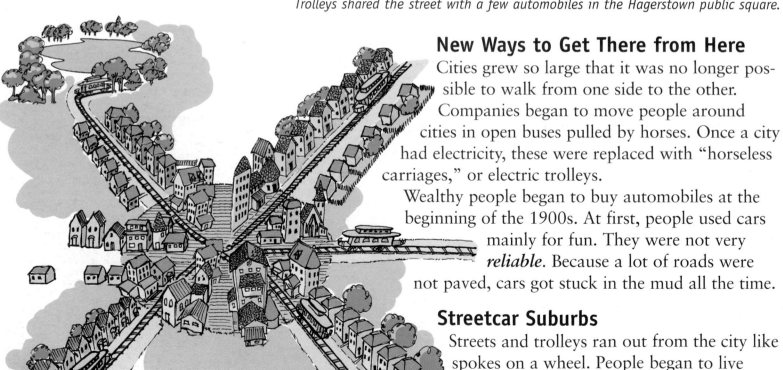

▲ Drawing by Ray Cornia

New Ways to Get There from Here

Cities grew so large that it was no longer possible to walk from one side to the other. Companies began to move people around cities in open buses pulled by horses. Once a city had electricity, these were replaced with "horseless carriages," or electric trolleys.

Wealthy people began to buy automobiles at the beginning of the 1900s. At first, people used cars mainly for fun. They were not very *reliable*. Because a lot of roads were not paved, cars got stuck in the mud all the time.

Streetcar Suburbs

Streets and trolleys ran out from the city like spokes on a wheel. People began to live along the "spokes" because they could get to work easily. They began to build *suburbs*. Sometimes people called them "streetcar suburbs."

To reach Ocean City, some people took a ferry boat across the bay and then a train across eastern Maryland.

Because most Maryland hotels only allowed white visitors, African Americans went to separate vacation spots. Here children are learning to swim at Carr's Beach.

Sunday in the Park

As the cities grew, people worried that there would be no open spaces left. They began to set aside large areas of land with trees, lakes, and nice grassy places for picnics. On Sundays, families often took a trolley car to the park to spend the day. There they could rent a boat or watch a baseball game. Once railroads, trolleys, and cars made it easier for people to travel, families began to travel for vacation.

THE RICH AND THE POOR

Wealthy families and poor families lived very differently. A few people made large fortunes in business and industry. Their families were the first to have running water, electricity, and cars.

There were more poor people than there were rich people. In cities, poor families often lived in buildings that had no running water. They used an outhouse and an outside pump for water. When they did get running water, several families shared a bathroom and a kitchen.

A lot of families were neither rich nor poor. They had good homes and enough to eat, but they were not wealthy.

The families in this building shared one water faucet.

In a one-room schoolhouse, children of all ages learned together. What does the picture tell you about life at this school?

This book wagon traveled around Washington County bringing books to readers in small towns.

GOING TO SCHOOL 100 YEARS AGO

By 1900, every county in Maryland had public schools. In small towns, most schools had just one or two rooms.

Schools across the state were *segregated*. White children and black children had to go to different schools. In many places, white schools got the newest buildings, books, and equipment. Schools for black children got the old things from the white schools, sometimes even the old buildings.

Many immigrant families did not know English when they first came to the United States. It was hard for children to learn when they could not understand what their teachers were saying.

Boys and girls who worked in factories and mines could not go to school. Their families needed the money they earned to buy food. Children of migrant farm workers did not go to school either. They worked all day in the fields and gave the money to their parents.

W h a t   d o   y o u   t h i n k ?

Do you think the school system in 1900 was fair to everyone?

WORKING TO MAKE THINGS BETTER

You have seen that the people faced lots of problems. Many men and women tried to solve these problems. They wanted to make life better for everyone. They worked very hard and made important changes. They wanted our country to make good progress, so they were called *Progressives*.

One way that we can change things is through *politics*. The people who make our laws are very important. Laws can make a real difference in how we all live. In the early 1900s, a lot of Progressives won elections. Then they were able to make laws.

The Progressives passed laws that required safety inspections in the factories. They made companies give their workers better pay. They passed laws saying that all children had to go to school. This got children out of dangerous factories and mines. An education also meant that the children would be able to get better jobs when they grew up.

Harry Cummings was the first African American on the Baltimore City Council.

The Power of Voting

Soon after the Civil War, African Americans were allowed to vote. In Annapolis, Baltimore, and Cambridge, black men were elected to city councils. They could help look out for the needs of the people in their communities.

Immigrants saw that it was very important to participate in our government. Many became American citizens so they could vote. Soon Irish, Italian, and Polish immigrants held government jobs. They could help make our laws.

Most progressives wanted women to be able to vote, too. But some men did not want women to be involved in politics. They thought women did not know enough to vote. Women and the men who supported them fought hard to get the right to vote.

Maryland women fought hard for the right to vote for their government leaders.

Labor Unions

Workers got together to help make their lives better. They formed *unions*. The unions demanded higher pay and safe working conditions. Union leaders talked to the people in the government and helped convince them to vote for these changes.

Volunteering Their Time and Money

A lot of people volunteered their time and talents to make life better. Women in Allegany County opened a soup kitchen to help feed the poor. Men and women in cities opened settlement houses. Settlement houses offered classes in cooking, sewing, English, and other important skills.

African American women and white women formed clubs. The clubs helped clean up the streets. They opened kindergartens and nurseries where working mothers could get care for their children. They fought to make water and milk safe to drink. They planned summer activities for city children. These women made a big difference in many people's lives.

Wealthy people who give their money to help others are called *philanthropists*. Some philanthropists in Maryland gave away their fortunes to build hospitals, universities, libraries, and museums. They wanted to help all the people in the state.

A merchant named Johns Hopkins gave his fortune to build a hospital and university. When he was young, Johns worked on the family farm. He did not have much time to go to school. People think that is why he thought education was so important.

Linking the past to the present

Volunteers did many things to make people's lives better around 1900. What kinds of things do volunteers do today?

Enoch Pratt gave his fortune to start a library that was free to all people. Many libraries admitted only white people. You can see in this picture from the 1930s that Pratt's gift was for everyone in Baltimore.

What Would You Bring?

Pretend you are moving to a foreign country. You must travel like the immigrants did 100 years ago. You can't pack much. You will be sailing on a boat with hundreds of strangers. There is hardly room for you, let alone your things. You must carry everything with you.

What do you choose? Imagine that you have a grocery bag. You can take only those things that will fit into the grocery bag. Make a list of what you will bring. Explain why you chose each item.

Discoveries and Inventions

What is the difference between a discovery and an invention? We discover things that we did not know about. We invent things that are new. Discoveries often lead to new inventions. For example:

- The discovery of steam power led to the invention of steam trains and steamships.
- The discovery of electricity led to the invention of electric lights, electric refrigerators, electric washing machines, and electric trolley cars.

Can you think of some other discoveries? Did they lead to new inventions?

Questions for Review

1. What is a century?

2. What are migrant workers? What kinds of jobs did they do on the farms?

3. What minerals found in Maryland were used in the new industries?

4. What was the Industrial Revolution?

5. List three goods made at factories in Maryland.

6. List five countries from which immigrants came to Maryland during this time.

7. List two new inventions that made life easier.

8. List two changes in transportation that helped people get from place to place.

9. Schools during this time were segregated. What does that mean?

10. What do we call someone who gives away money to help other people?

Geography Tie-In

Find out what was on the same land as your school 100 years ago. Do the same with your home or shopping mall. How was the same land used 100 years ago?

chapter 8

THE TIME
1900–1945

PEOPLE TO KNOW
President Woodrow Wilson
Eubie Blake
Cab Calloway
Babe Ruth
Roy Campanella
Junior Gilliam
Mary Risteau
President Franklin Roosevelt
Lillie Carroll Jackson
Adolf Hitler

PLACES TO LOCATE
Baltimore
England
France
Russia
Germany
Austria
Turkey
Washington, D.C.
Greenbelt
Japan
Poland
China
Pearl Harbor, Hawaii
Italy
Hagerstown

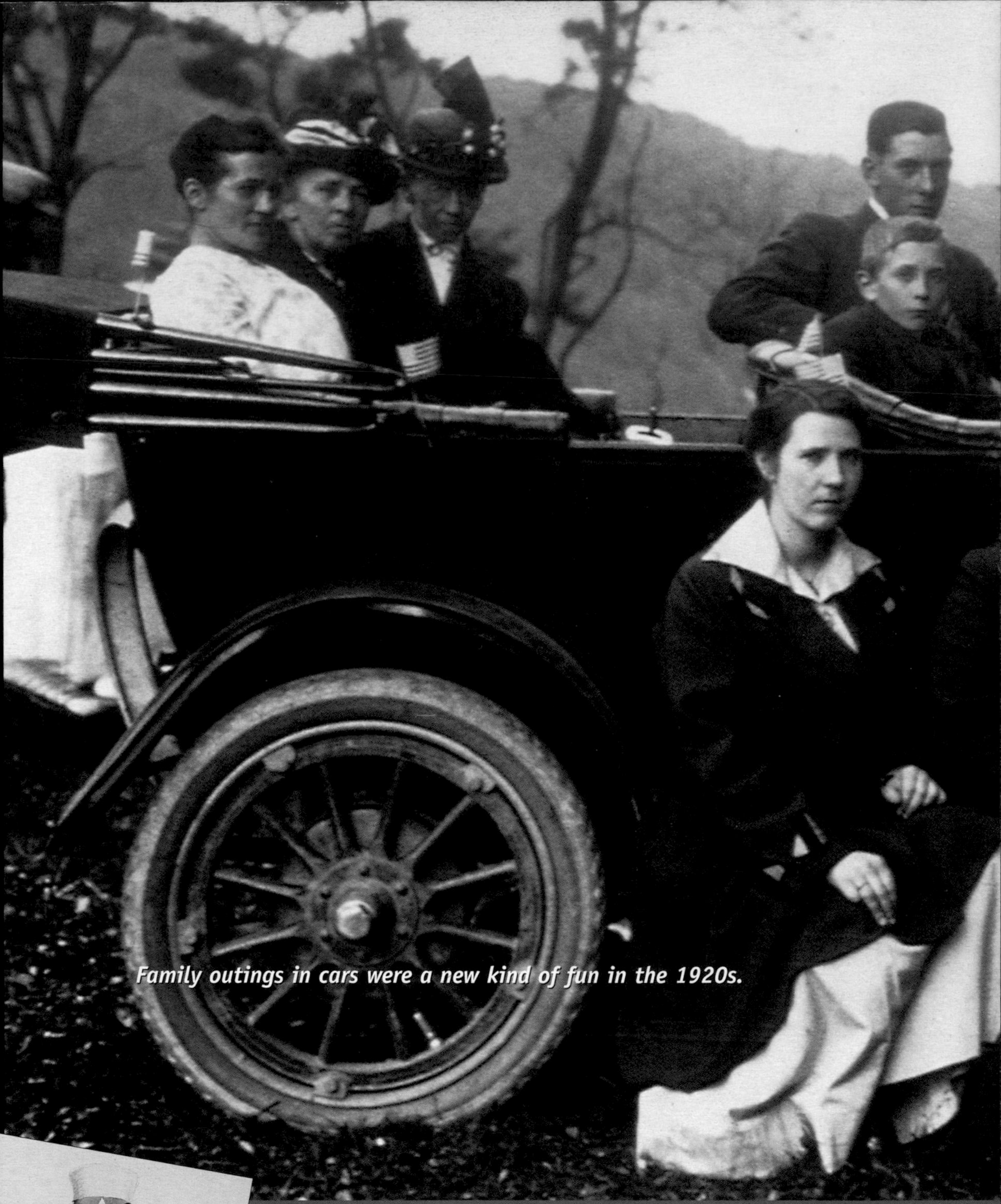
Family outings in cars were a new kind of fun in the 1920s.

timeline of events

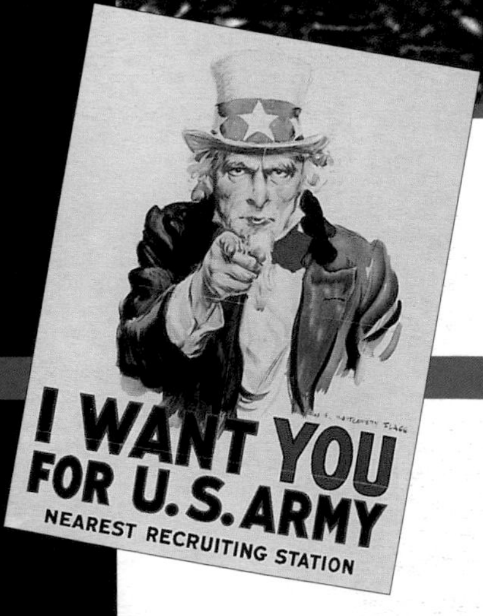
I WANT YOU
FOR U.S. ARMY
NEAREST RECRUITING STATION

1914–1918
World War I
The U.S. enters the war in 1917.

1915

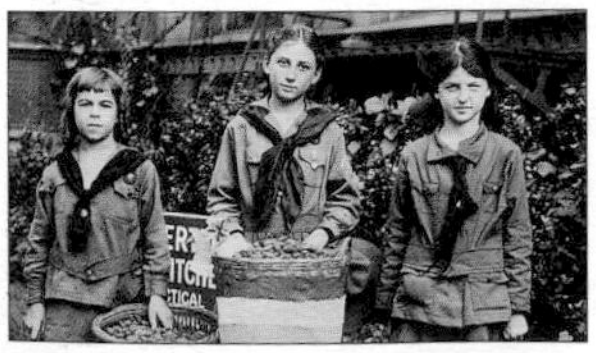

1920s
The Roaring Twenties
The Great Migration

1920
Women win the right to vote.

1920

1921
Mary Risteau is the first woman to serve in the Maryland House of Delegates.

19

chapter 8

Taking Our Place in the World

TERMS TO UNDERSTAND
raw materials
lynch
renaissance
prohibit
depression
stock
dictator
ration
holocaust
concentration camp
atom

1930s
The Great Depression

1941
December 7
The Japanese bomb Pearl Harbor, Hawaii.
The U.S. enters World War II.

1930   1935   1940   1945

1929
The stock market crashes.

1939–1945
World War II

1919–1933
Liquor is banned in the United States.

Soldiers paraded through downtown Baltimore before going "over there."

THE WORLD GOES TO WAR

FAST STEAMSHIPS, TELEPHONES, and radios were helping Marylanders connect with people from faraway places. For better and for worse, Maryland was drawn into events that were happening all around the world.

A terrible war broke out in Europe in 1914. The countries in Europe took sides. England, France, and Russia joined together and supported each other. They fought against Germany, Austria, and Turkey.

At first, Americans wanted to stay out of the war. War is a horrible thing. It kills and wounds soldiers and other people.

People called the war in Europe the "Great War." We now call it World War I.

The United States Goes to War

Our country was shipping food, *raw materials*, and weapons to help England and France. When German submarines started to attack these ships, Americans got angry. Some Americans said we should go to war. Other Americans said we should not.

President Woodrow Wilson believed we should fight. Congress declared war against Germany and its allies. Soldiers from Maryland soon were on the front lines in Europe.

Maryland Does Its Part

Marylanders helped in the war effort. Women's clubs made bandages. Families planted "victory gardens" to help grow more food. They turned their lights off early to save fuel.

When the men left for war, they left their jobs behind. Someone had to do the work. Women moved into new types of work to take their place. They worked in factories, as telephone operators, and on the streetcars and railroads.

Factories were busy making guns, tanks, ships, and other goods for the war. People moved from rural areas into cities to work in war industries. African Americans from southern states came to live and work in Maryland.

The War Ends

Peace came when Germany surrendered on November 11, 1918. The news that the war was over arrived by telegraph.

In Maryland and across the nation, everyone celebrated. Towns held parades to honor the soldiers. The troops marched through the streets as the people cheered. November 11 is now celebrated as Veteran's Day.

Posters urged everyone to help in the war effort. What does Uncle Sam—in his red, white, and blue—stand for?

Over 60,000 men and women from Maryland served in the army and navy.

Girl Scouts collected peach pits for the war effort. The pits were turned into charcoal. Charcoal was used in gas masks to filter out poisonous gas.

Problems After the War

During World War I, life had changed for many Americans. People from small towns had moved into cities. More women than ever before had gone to work outside the home. Many people did not return to the way of life they had before the war.

When peace returned, the factories that made things like guns and army boots closed down. There were not enough jobs for the soldiers coming home. Many soldiers wanted to buy a home and start a family, but there were not enough homes to go around. People were very angry.

The Ku Klux Klan

A group called the Ku Klux Klan said that African Americans, Catholics, Jews, and immigrants were the cause of America's problems. They attacked immigrant workers. Angry mobs surrounded the homes of innocent African American families. They set fire to the homes. Sometimes they took the father of a family away and *lynched* him. That means they killed him by hanging him from a tree.

Klan members wore white hoods to hide their faces. They did not want people to know who they were. They wanted to scare people. Most people in Maryland and across the country thought the Klan was very un-American. They did not like the bad things it did.

The Maryland Adventure

THE ROARING TWENTIES

After a few years, new industries made new jobs. Rural families got electric power for the first time. They could tune in to radio shows, keep food in a refrigerator, and put away the gas lamps.

Many families bought their first car during the 1920s. Cars gave people freedom to go wherever they wanted to go.

People wanted to forget about the war and just have fun. A new type of music called jazz was popular. So were lively dances such as the "Charleston." Musicians, artists, and writers tried out wonderful new styles. Marylanders were part of the new culture.

The Harlem Renaissance

In big cities like Baltimore, Washington, and New York, there were many African American musicians, writers, and artists. They were part of a movement called the Harlem Renaissance. (A *renaissance* is a new beginning, or rebirth.) Eubie Blake and Cab Calloway were famous jazz musicians from Maryland. People from all over Maryland traveled to Baltimore and Washington when these famous musicians performed.

New fashions and dances were part of the Roaring Twenties.

The Great Migration

Many African Americans moved from farms and towns in the South to cities in the North. People left the South for several reasons. States there had taken away black people's right to vote. Some whites had used violence to keep them out of good jobs and decent homes. It was hard to get a good education. Most libraries and parks were segregated. Many people left the South to get away from all the problems.

In the North, jobs in industry paid good salaries. Black people could vote. Schools were better and public places were open to all people. This move from the rural South to the cities of the North is called the Great Migration.

Eubie Blake

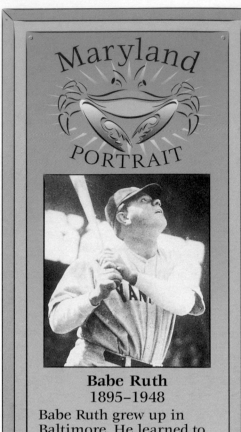
Sports

Many people in Maryland cheered for professional sports teams. Baseball was especially popular. The great player Babe Ruth got his start with the Baltimore Orioles.

Like so many parts of life, baseball teams were segregated. There was a separate Negro League. Roy Campanella and Junior Gilliam played for the Baltimore Elite Giants. They went on to play in the Major Leagues.

Women Win the Right to Vote

From the colonial days when Margaret Brent had first tried to vote in the Maryland General Assembly, women had fought for this basic right. Finally, in 1920, the female half of America's population won the right to vote.

Mary Risteau was voted in as the first woman in the Maryland House of Delegates.

Prohibition

The 1920s was a decade with a lot of fun and excitement, but it was also a time of crime and violence. One reason was liquor. In 1919 the United States made it illegal to make or sell liquor. This was called Prohibition, because the government *prohibited* people from making and selling liquor.

People who still wanted to drink went to "speakeasies," or secret clubs where they could buy liquor. Gangsters often supplied the liquor. "Bootlegging" (making and selling liquor secretly) became big business.

Prohibition did not last long. Liquor was made legal again in 1933.

Eleven members of the Bettinger family lived in this small cabin. They put on their best clothes for the picture.

THE GREAT DEPRESSION

A *depression* is a time when many people can't make enough money to take care of their families. They want to work, but they can't find jobs. The depression of the 1930s was the worst depression the United States has ever known. That is why it is called the Great Depression.

People couldn't afford to buy more radios and cars. They stopped buying new homes. This meant that factories did not need to make as much, so they sent workers home. Without paychecks, workers could no longer buy things. More businesses slowed down.

Some people had bought *stocks*. A stock is a piece of a company. As companies stopped making goods, the value of their stock went down very quickly. People said that the stock market had crashed.

Some banks had put money in stocks. When the stock market crashed, the banks ran out of money. When people went to their banks to get their money, it wasn't there. Many people lost every penny they had saved.

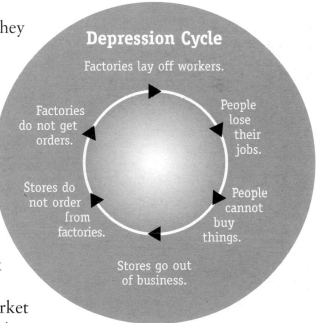

Depression Cycle

Factories lay off workers.

People lose their jobs.

People cannot buy things.

Stores go out of business.

Stores do not order from factories.

Factories do not get orders.

How People Survived

Men sold apples on street corners to earn money. People stood in long lines to get free soup and bread. They grew gardens in their backyards. They mended old clothes again and again to try to make them last. They put cardboard in the bottom of their shoes when the soles got holes.

Many families lost their homes. Some people lived under bridges or made shelters out of scrap wood or metal. Many moved in with relatives.

People tried to help each other as much as they could. Soup kitchens opened to serve free meals to hungry people. Local police and firemen collected food and gave it to families that had no money.

Minorities and Women during the Depression

During this troubled time, some companies fired black workers before they fired white workers. Women were often fired before men were. This was not fair, but this was what happened. It was one form of discrimination.

African Americans organized protests. Groups such as the National Association for the Advancement of Colored People (NAACP) had many members in Maryland. They led men and women in protests to make things more equal.

Can you tell from the sign why these women are marching? They are urging people in the African Amercian community to shop only in stores where they are allowed to work.

People knew that Roosevelt had overcome polio, a disease that left many children and adults unable to walk. They knew that Roosevelt was a fighter. They believed that if he could overcome polio, he could also overcome the depression.

THE NEW DEAL

People began to wonder if the depression would ever end. They were worried that life would just get worse and worse. People in the government decided that they must take action.

President Franklin Roosevelt had a plan. He called his plan the New Deal. He started projects in order to create jobs. The government hired people to do all sorts of work.

Alphabet Soup

The Civilian Conservation Corps (CCC) put young men to work building and repairing parks across the country. They planted trees. They built golf courses, playgrounds, and hiking trails.

The Works Progress Administration (WPA) put men and a few women to work building new schools, post offices, roads, and bridges. Artists painted murals on the walls. The WPA paid actors to put on shows. It hired history experts to write local histories. Writers collected stories from people who had been slaves and wrote them down so they would not be forgotten.

The Farm Security Administration (FSA) helped farmers. FSA workers traveled to farms across Maryland and the nation, teaching modern ways of farming. They also gave health and safety information.

So many government agencies were known by their initials that people called them "alphabet soup." Thousands and thousands of people worked for the government.

Some people were unhappy that the government had grown so large. However, most people were happy that the government was trying to help people get jobs.

The FSA helped this farmer. His water well was too close to the barnyard. The animal waste went down through the dirt into the water. The water made people sick. The FSA loaned the farmer money to put in a safer well.

Linking the past to the present

One of the New Deal programs helped older Americans. It was called Social Security. Part of the money people earned would go to retired people. Then, when those workers retired, they would get social security money too. Today, many Marylanders work for the Department of Social Security.

Greenbelt

Because of all the new government programs, many people came to work in Washington, D.C. They needed a place to live. Families moved into the regions of Maryland that were near the nation's capital.

Thousands of people got jobs building the new town of Greenbelt. It was just twelve miles from Washington, D.C.

New Deal planners wanted the town to be close to jobs and have lots of parks for people to enjoy. They built a town center with a school, library, shops, and entertainment. Greenbelt was a model for many planned towns that were built later.

Greenbelt

Americans went to Europe and Asia to fight in World War II.

A SECOND WORLD WAR

While Americans were suffering through the depression, so were people in many other countries. President Roosevelt and the New Deal helped Americans get through those difficult years. Not all countries were so lucky.

In some places, *dictators* took over the government. A dictator is a ruler who has all of the power. Adolf Hitler was the dictator of Germany. Italy also had a dictator. The dictators stopped holding elections. They killed people who were against them. In Japan, the army took over the government.

The rulers of these countries wanted to conquer their neighbors. When the German army invaded Poland, all of Europe went to war. On the other side of the world, Japan invaded China.

Attack at Pearl Harbor!

The United States did not get involved in the war for the first two years. Then something terrible happened in Hawaii.

The U.S. Navy had a base in Pearl Harbor, Hawaii. One day in December, Japanese airplanes dropped bombs on the navy base. The bombs destroyed ships and killed people.

During World War II, posters urged black and white workers and soldiers to come together.

The next day, the United States declared war on Japan. Japan had an agreement with Germany and Italy. They agreed that if one country got into war against the United States, the others would join in too.

Once again we were at war. We were fighting against Germany, Italy, and Japan. On our side were England, France, Russia, and China.

Air raid sirens were built to warn people if enemy planes were spotted. During drills, people practiced running to bomb shelters.

Service in the army was a matter of pride for Maryland's African Americans.

Troops from Maryland

Maryland sent over 240,000 men and women to serve in the war. Soldiers and sailors fought in countries around the world. They fought on ships in both the Atlantic and Pacific Oceans.

Maryland also sent medical units to the war. Doctors and nurses from Johns Hopkins, the University of Maryland, Provident Hospital, and many others took care of wounded soldiers and sailors.

Guarding the Homefront

Guards were posted all along Maryland's beaches. Their job was to watch for German ships. German submarines did come very close to the shore. If you drive into Delaware, just north of Ocean City, you can see concrete towers where the guards stood watch.

Because modern airplanes could fly across the ocean and new bombs could go long distances, states along the Atlantic Coast feared an air attack by the Germans. Families hung blackout shades on their windows. This was in case an enemy pilot flew by. If he could not see any lights, he would think no one was there. Local volunteers patrolled every neighborhood to make sure people were following the blackout rules.

Rationing

To be sure that the soldiers had everything they needed, the government limited what people at home could buy. People could buy only so much sugar, meat, butter, coffee, gas, and tires. Each family was given *ration* stamps every month. When the stamps ran out, the family had to wait until the next month to buy more items.

UNITED STATES OF AMERICA
OFFICE OF PRICE ADMINISTRATION

RATION COUPON
FOR
FIVE
POINTS

PROCESSED FOODS

OPA Form R-1324

This woman fastened airplane wings at the Fairchild Aircraft Factory in Hagerstown.

Help from Home

It was important to give our soldiers and sailors everything they needed to fight. Maryland played a big role in producing ships and airplanes for the troops. Once again, women did their part. Before World War II ended, over 50,000 men and women worked in the aircraft industry. Even more men and women built ships.

The Glenn L. Martin Company made bomber planes.

Taking Our Place in the World

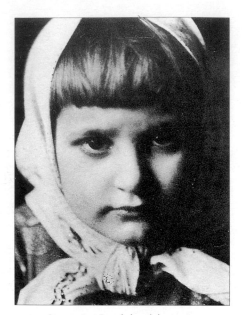

A young Jewish girl wrote:

"Next year would have been my last year at school, but I won't be able to graduate . . . the schools have closed. . . . The Nazis have forced more than 5,000 Jews in Minsk [Russia] . . . to live in one small area of town."

The Holocaust

One terrible thing that happened during World War II was the *Holocaust.* Adolf Hitler believed that Germans were better than other kinds of people. He believed the world would be better without all different kinds of people. He especially hated Jews. First he took away their rights. Then he decided to kill the Jews in all the countries he conquered.

Hitler's troops rounded up all the Jewish people they could find. They put them into railroad cars and sent them to *concentration camps.* At the camps, there was hardly anything to eat. The people were forced to do hard labor until they died. People who were too old, too young, or too weak to work were murdered. About six million Jews died in these camps. So did six million other people.

When the war ended, American soldiers went to free the people in the concentration camps. They were horrified at what they saw. The survivors looked like walking skeletons. Entire families had been wiped out. Some survivors spent a lifetime looking for lost relatives and friends.

THE END OF WORLD WAR II

After years of fighting and millions of deaths, World War II finally ended. The United States and its allies invaded and defeated Germany. Japan fought on for several more months.

The Atomic Bomb

During the war, countries on both sides had tried to build a super bomb. The United States and Britain succeeded first. They won the race when scientists figured out how to split an *atom.* This made a new kind of energy called atomic energy. The scientists used this energy to make the world's first atomic bomb.

To end the war with Japan, the U.S. dropped an atomic bomb on Hiroshima, Japan. Japan did not surrender. After the U.S. dropped a second bomb on another city, Japan surrendered.

Peace at Last

The war was over. People in Maryland and across the country celebrated. They were glad to see peace return. Everyone looked forward to better days.

Searching for the Answers—Your Own Interview

Interview someone who lived during the Great Depression or World War II.

Before the interview, get together with other students in your class and make a list of questions you would like the person to answer. Here are some suggestions:

Do you remember the Great Depression?
• Was anyone in your family out of work?
• What things were hard to do without much money?

Do you remember World War II?
• Did you or anyone you knew fight in the army or navy? Where?
• Did you know anyone who was injured or killed in the war?

Questions for Review

1. What kinds of things did Marylanders do to help the country during World War I?

2. Who stepped in to do the men's jobs when they went off to war?

3. Why do we celebrate Veteran's Day on November 11?

4. What kinds of things did people do for fun during the Roaring Twenties?

5. What was the Great Migration? Why did it happen?

6. Who was Babe Ruth?

7. What was the name of President Roosevelt's plan to help end the depression?

8. List three government agencies that gave people jobs.

9. What event caused the United States to enter World War II?

10. What was the Holocaust?

Geography Tie-In

On a map of the world, find the countries that helped us win World War II. Then find the countries we fought against during the war.

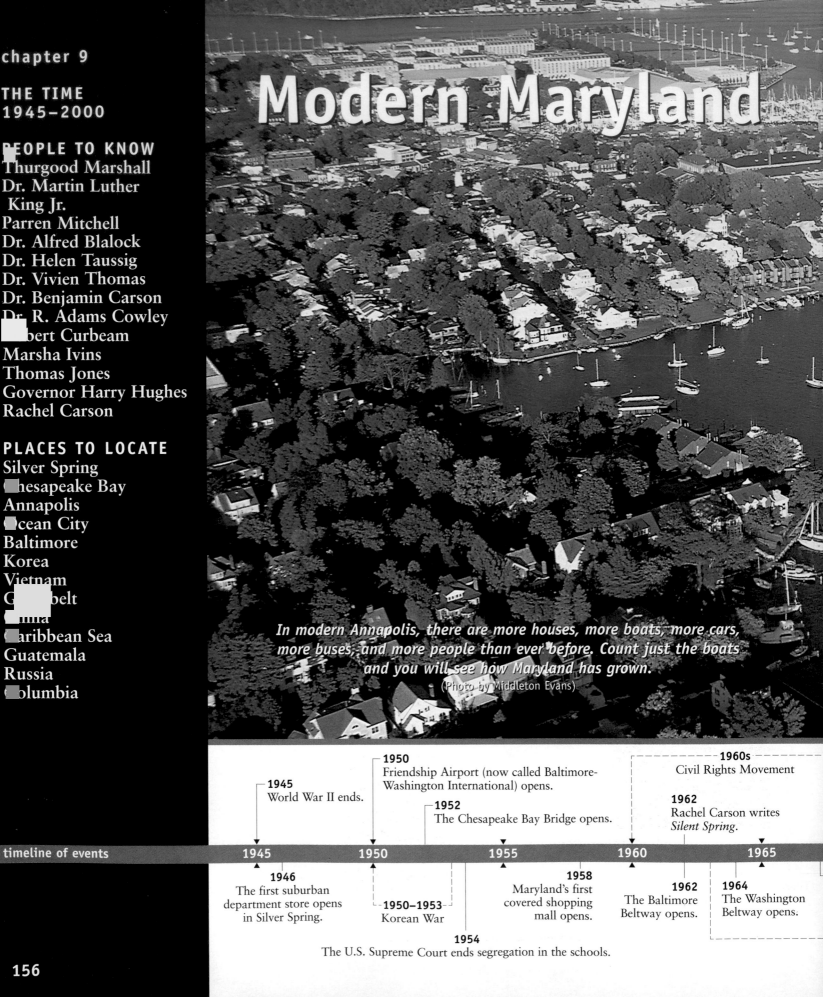

PEOPLE TO KNOW
Thurgood Marshall
Dr. Martin Luther
 King Jr.
Parren Mitchell
Dr. Alfred Blalock
Dr. Helen Taussig
Dr. Vivien Thomas
Dr. Benjamin Carson
Dr. R. Adams Cowley
▮bert Curbeam
Marsha Ivins
Thomas Jones
Governor Harry Hughes
Rachel Carson

PLACES TO LOCATE
Silver Spring
▮hesapeake Bay
Annapolis
▮cean City
Baltimore
Korea
Vietnam
G▮▮belt
▮▮▮▮
▮aribbean Sea
Guatemala
Russia
▮olumbia

Modern Maryland

In modern Annapolis, there are more houses, more boats, more cars, more buses, and more people than ever before. Count just the boats and you will see how Maryland has grown.
(Photo by Middleton Evans)

timeline of events

1945
World War II ends.

1946
The first suburban
department store opens
in Silver Spring.

1950
Friendship Airport (now called Baltimore-
Washington International) opens.

1950–1953
Korean War

1952
The Chesapeake Bay Bridge opens.

1954
The U.S. Supreme Court ends segregation in the schools.

1958
Maryland's first
covered shopping
mall opens.

1960s
Civil Rights Movement

1962
Rachel Carson writes
Silent Spring.

1962
The Baltimore
Beltway opens.

1964
The Washington
Beltway opens.

1945   1950   1955   1960   1965

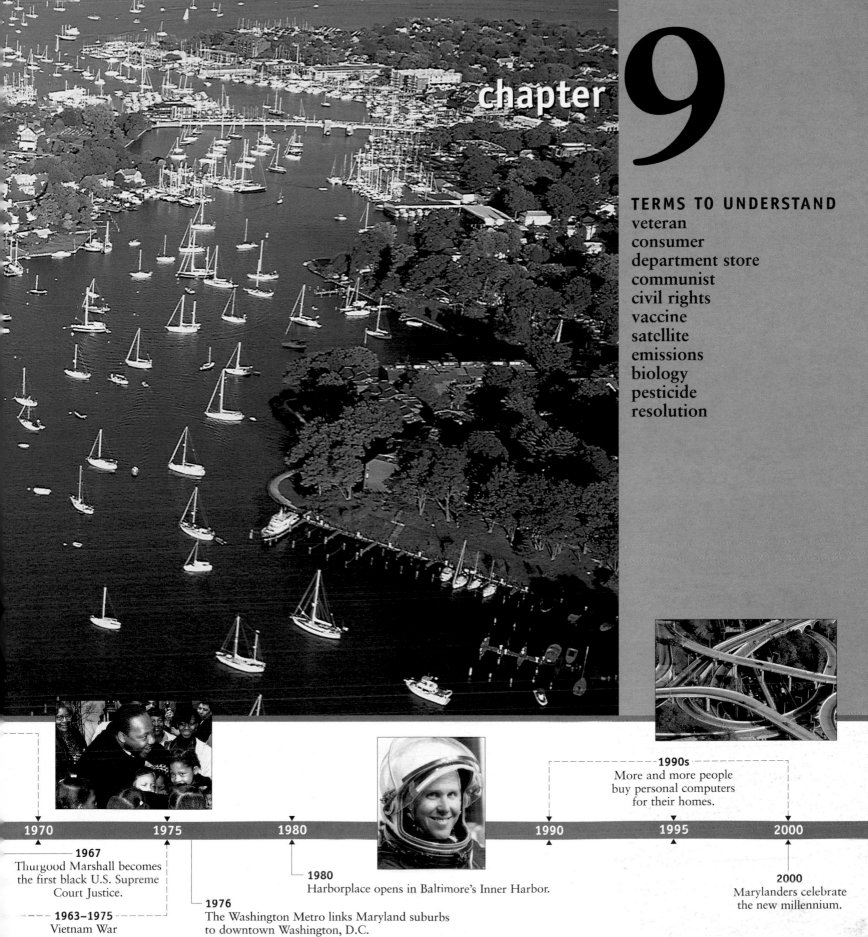

chapter

9

1990s
More and more people
buy personal computers
for their homes.

1970   1975   1980   1990   1995   2000

1967
Thurgood Marshall becomes
the first black U.S. Supreme
Court Justice.

1963–1975
Vietnam War

1976
The Washington Metro links Maryland suburbs
to downtown Washington, D.C.

1980
Harborplace opens in Baltimore's Inner Harbor.

2000
Marylanders celebrate
the new millennium.

Crowds came to downtown Baltimore to celebrate the end of World War II. What does the electric sign on the corner of the building say?

COMING HOME

AFTER WORLD WAR II, thousands of men and women came home to Maryland. They had served their country in many parts of the world. Now they could be with their families again.

To say "thank you" for the years of service, the government paid for education for everyone who had served in the Armed Forces. This was called the G.I. Bill of Rights. *Veterans* could go to state colleges such as Frostburg, Morgan, Salisbury, and Towson. They could go to medical school at the University of Maryland or Johns Hopkins. They could learn to be a carpenter, plumber, or mechanic. They could learn the skills they needed to get a good job.

Maryland industries went back to making products for *consumers*. After people finished school, there were plenty of jobs for them.

THE BUILDING BOOM

When the soldiers came home from the war, a lot of them wanted to get married and start a family. They needed homes. Companies began to build houses as soon as they could get enough wood, bricks, and pipes.

Families wanted space for their children to play. Builders put many of the new houses in the suburbs. They built roads and homes in the open land between the major streets and trolley car routes. When that land was full, they built further out in the country.

Problems in the Cities and Suburbs

Before long, companies followed the people to the suburbs. Many good jobs were no longer downtown. As more families bought cars, cities ran fewer trolleys and buses. Soon it was hard to get around if you didn't have a car. It took money to buy the new houses, so many of the people who stayed in the cities were poor.

When people moved away, the cities got less money in taxes. Soon the cities did not have enough money to pay for top-quality schools. Crime was a problem too. More people moved out of the cities to escape crime. Once these troubles began, it was hard to turn things around.

Many of the new suburbs passed rules like keeping your grass cut. Some made rules about who could buy a house in the community. Many of the new suburbs would not let African Americans or Jews buy houses. In other parts of the country, people from Asia and people who spoke Spanish could not live in certain neighborhoods.

Supermarkets and Shopping Malls

Instead of walking to the small grocery store at the corner, people drove to new "supermarkets" in the suburbs. Supermarkets had to have parking lots for all the cars. Today we see parking lots everywhere. Can you imagine a time when parking lots were a new thing?

The Hecht Company opened Maryland's first suburban *department store* in Silver Spring. Soon many stores opened branches in the suburbs. A few years later, Harundale Mall was built. It was the first covered shopping mall in the state.

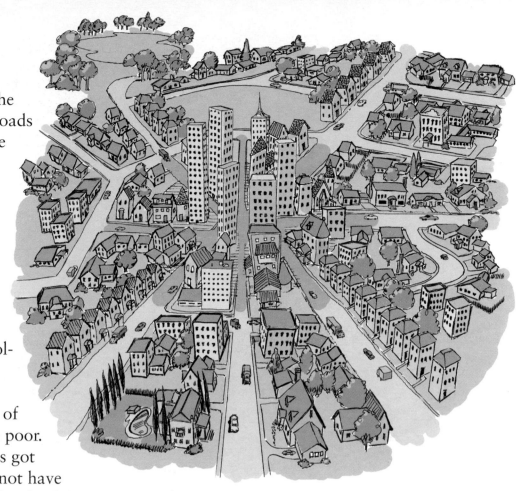

In the 1950s, builders put roads and homes in the open land between the major streets. When that land was full, they built further out in the country. Compare this drawing to the one on page 134.

Silver Spring

High-speed entrances and exits let people onto the wide highways. People laughed when they first saw pictures of these roads. They never dreamed they would drive on them one day.

▲ Photo by Middleton Evans

The Chesapeake Bay Bridge opened in 1952. It is over four miles long. Have you ever driven across the bay?

New Roads for New Cars

Maryland built new roads for all the new cars. The federal government spent a lot of money on new highways that went from state to state, all across the country. Many people got jobs building the highways. Highways had many lanes and no stop-lights so cars could go faster and cover long distances quickly.

Two important new roads connected suburbs around the cities. They were the Baltimore Beltway and the Washington Beltway.

The Chesapeake Bay Bridge

A new bridge near Annapolis connected the Eastern Shore and the Western Shore. The bridge changed the Eastern Shore forever. People built large stores, motels, and gas stations on land that had been covered with farms. Ocean City became a crowded resort. Weekend traffic jams were more and more common.

▲ Photo by M.E. Warren

Air Travel

Before World War II, most people did not travel on airplanes. Today, we fly across the country and around the world for business, vacations, and to visit friends and family.

Maryland's largest airport opened in 1950. It was named Friendship Airport. Today we call it the Baltimore-Washington International Airport, or BWI.

The Maryland Adventure

Do your grandparents remember getting their first televison?

POPULAR INVENTIONS

Cars and planes were not the only things that changed people's lives. Other inventions that we take for granted today came into use after World War II.

Most families started buying televisions in the 1950s. At first, TV programs were on for only a few hours each day. All the shows were in black and white. *I Love Lucy* was a popular comedy. Have you ever watched the re-runs?

> **W h a t   d o   y o u   t h i n k ?**
>
> After televisions came air conditioners, VCRs, computers, and cellular phones. In what ways, good and bad, have these things changed our lives?

"I was in first grade when my family got our first television set. That was in 1949. I was the second person in my class to have a TV. One morning a week there were two shows for children. My whole class would walk to my house or to my friend's house to see the shows. Our mothers gave everyone a lollipop or cookies. Everyone was very excited to see TV shows and to get out of school."

—*Sue Ellery*

WAR IN KOREA

In the early 1950s, the United States sent soldiers to Korea. Korea had been divided into two parts. North Korea had a *communist* government. South Korea's government was an ally of the United States.

When North Korea invaded South Korea, many nations sent troops to help South Korea. The United States was one of those nations. Soldiers from Maryland fought in the Korean War. After several years of war, the two sides agreed to stop fighting. Korea was still divided into two parts, but Maryland's men and women could return home.

Maryland PORTRAIT

Thurgood Marshall
1908–1993

Thurgood Marshall was born in Baltimore. He became a lawyer. He believed that the law should treat people equally and give justice to all Americans.

Thurgood Marshall argued a very famous case before the U.S. Supreme Court. The case was about whether it was legal to send black children and white children to separate schools. Marshall said that black children were not getting equal treatment. The justices agreed that separate schools went against the Constitution. Marshall had made a very powerful case.

Marshall became the first African American to serve on the United States Supreme Court.

Martin Luther King Jr. led peaceful protests for civil rights.

THE CIVIL RIGHTS MOVEMENT

In Maryland, as in many states, schools were segregated. The black schools did not have many things that the white schools had. They usually did not have new buildings or new books. Some did not have science labs or gyms.

Many jobs were closed to African Americans. Many hotels, restaurants, theaters, and even parks would not admit black families. In some theaters, blacks had to sit in the balcony.

Many Americans thought it was wrong to discriminate against people because of their race. More and more people, black and white, began to speak out for equality. They fought for *civil rights*. Civil rights are the basic rights that every citizen of our country is supposed to have. Children joined adults and college students in marches and protests until a new Maryland law opened public places to people of all races.

Lawyers went to court and said that black students should not have to go to separate schools. They said the black schools were not equal to the white schools. In 1954, the Supreme Court ruled that keeping blacks in separate schools was against the law. For the first time in Maryland's history, black and white children could go to school together.

Violence in the Streets

Despite the new laws, some white people refused to treat black people well. Black people became more and more frustrated. Life was not good in the inner cities, especially in black communities. No law had solved that problem. Civil rights workers now turned to the problem of poverty. Sometimes their protests ended in violence.

Dr. Martin Luther King Jr. was a famous civil rights leader. He led people in peaceful protests. Sadly, Dr. King was assassinated.

Americans were shocked and sad. Many were angry that Dr. King was killed just because he was trying to solve the problems of discrimination and poverty. In Baltimore and other cities, people took to the streets to show their sadness and anger.

Parren Mitchell used politics to fight for equality. He was elected as Maryland's first black congressman in 1970.

WAR IN VIETNAM

During the 1960s, the United States became involved in a very long war. The country of Vietnam was divided into two parts, just as Korea had been. North Vietnam had a communist government. South Vietnam's government was an ally of the United States.

When a civil war broke out, our country sent troops to help the South. Men and women from Maryland were called to fight in a country far away.

Some Americans saw the Vietnam War as a fight for freedom. Other Americans believed that we had no business in Vietnam. They thought we needed to solve the problems in our own country instead of sending our soldiers so far away.

People who were against the war marched in the streets. Sometimes the protests became violent. After ten years, our government brought the soldiers home.

The Vietnam Veterans' Memorial in Washington, D.C., is a big, black, granite wall. It lists the names of the men and women who gave their lives in the Vietman War.

MARYLAND MEDICINE

Do you dread getting shots? They may hurt for a second, but shots are good for you! They protect you from major diseases. Doctors in Maryland helped to develop new *vaccines*, or shots, for polio, measles, and rubella.

Over the last fifty years, many important medical treatments have been discovered in Maryland. Our universities, hospitals, and research centers have become known around the world.

Helicopters bring patients to the Shock Trauma Center at the University of Maryland Hospital for quick treatment.

▲ Photo of helicopter by Middleton Evans

Doctors Helping Children

Many doctors from Maryland are known around the world for their work with children. Here are a few stories about modern medical pioneers.

In the past, babies born with certain heart problems usually died. A team at Johns Hopkins Hospital figured out a way to help them. Dr. Alfred Blalock, Dr. Helen Taussig, and Dr. Vivien Thomas found a way to open up a baby's chest and operate on the heart. Their work has saved thousands of babies' lives.

At the same hospital, Dr. Benjamin Carson performs operations on children's brains. He has operated on children from around the world and has saved many lives.

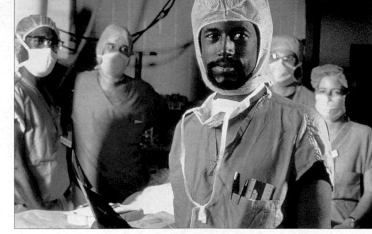

Dr. Benjamin Carson became famous around the world when he separated twins who were born joined at the head.

The Shock Trauma Center

At the University of Maryland Hospital, Dr. R. Adams Cowley and his team worked on the problem of how to treat severely injured patients. They started the Shock Trauma Center to help victims of car accidents, shootings, and other severe injuries.

Dr. Cowley discovered that patients getting treatment within one "golden hour" often lived, while patients who did not get rapid treatment were likely to die. His techniques have saved thousands of lives.

Maryland in Space

A t the Goddard Space Flight Center in Greenbelt, scientists research where to build rocket and *satellite* systems. The center is part of the National Aeronautics and Space Administration, or NASA.

Have you ever looked through a telescope? Did you see stars and planets? One of the most powerful telescopes is the Hubble Space Telescope. It was developed by scientists at the Space Telescope Science Institute in Maryland.

Maryland Astronauts

Robert Curbeam studied at the U.S. Naval Academy in Annapolis. He was selected by NASA for the astronaut program in 1994. Curbeam's first mission in space lasted for twelve days. He orbitted the earth 189 times and travelled 4.7 million miles. When he is not flying, Robert Curbeam enjoys biking, weightlifting, and spending time with his family.

Marsha Ivins has spent over 1,000 hours in space on four flights. She has helped to put satellites in position. On one flight, she docked with the Russian space station *Mir*. The mission was to exchange crews. The crew also moved food, water, experiment equipment, and samples between the two spacccraft. For fun, Marsha Ivins flies airplanes and bakes.

Thomas Jones helped set a shuttle record by spending nearly eighteen days in orbit around the earth. He flew as a mission special-ist. During his three trips, he has spent over forty days in space. In his free time, Jones enjoys reading, baseball, hiking, biking, camping, skiing, and flying.

The Hubble Space Telescope is so strong that we can see millions of miles through space, millions of light years away!

New Marylanders

Over time, people from many different lands have come to live in Maryland. Our newest immigrants are coming from all over the world.

Many people come here from countries that do not have the freedoms we enjoy. They want freedom of speech and freedom of religion. They want a good education and good jobs. Let's meet a few modern immigrants.

Anni and Laiza Braine

Beverly and Hayden Braine have made two trips to China. Each time they brought home a little girl. Anni (right) came to Maryland when she was eighteen months old. When she grew older and learned her own history, she wanted her parents to adopt another little girl. All three went on the long plane trip to China. Now Anni helps take care of her little sister Laiza.

In China, there are many children, especially girls, in orphanages. Their parents have died, or were unable to take care of their babies. Beverly and Hayden Braine were very happy to find their new daughters. They give them lots of love, plenty to eat, a safe home, and a good education. In recent years, many Americans have made children from other countries part of their families.

Mariette Danielle Phillips

Mariette Danielle Phillips' parents came from islands in the Caribbean Sea. What does she think of Maryland?

My father is a university professor of history. He first came here to study. My mother is the [accountant] of an engineering company. She also was a student when she came here. I was born . . . in Montgomery County. Now I am a freshman at Takoma Academy. We live in Silver Spring along with our pet bird and dog.

Sometimes we visit our family in the Caribbean. . . . Everyone on those islands speaks English. It is fun to travel there and visit my family. I think Maryland is a small but beautiful state with many friendly citizens who, like my parents, came from other countries and chose to make Maryland their home.

Dasha and Grisha Iventichev

Dasha (left) and Grisha (right) Iventichev are twins. They are ten years old. They came to Maryland from Russia in 2000. Both Dasha and Grisha studied English in Russia.

Dasha: *When we arrived, everybody was friendly. I had nice friends right away. I think school is easy. I like Girl Scouts and singing in a choir. I like having my own room. There is lots more stuff here than in Russia. I have lots of clothes.*

One thing that is different here is that we can see squirrels and rabbits and chipmunks. In Russia, those animals live in the woods.

Grisha: *School is easier here. But it is hard to speak English. The food is different. There are no pizzas or tacos in Russia. In the fall, I played soccer. In the winter, I played basketball. Now I am playing baseball. Sometimes I am the pitcher. We went to see an Orioles game the first week in the season. It was the first baseball game I had seen.*

Mary Valladares

Mary Valladares (second from left) came to this country from Guatemala when she was twelve years old.

When I arrived, I knew very little English. I could say "hello" and "goodbye" and I could count to ten. At first, school was very difficult. Two girls beat me up because I looked different and spoke a different language. It took me about a year and a half until I could do everything in English. We spoke Spanish at home. I was the first person in my family to finish high school and college.

My brothers came after I did. . . . In Guatemala, there was a civil war. The army would come through the small towns and take away all the teenage boys. They forced them to become soldiers. My parents wanted my brothers to come here so they would not be killed.

I married a man whose ancestors are Polish and German. We have two children. I fix Polish foods, and my family eats Latin American foods too. In America, we all come from different backgrounds. The world is shrinking. It is important for us to learn about each other.

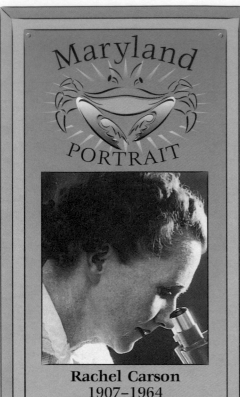
Rachel Carson
1907–1964

Rachel Carson was trained in *biology* (a science that studies living things) at the Johns Hopkins University. In the 1950s, she learned that a lot of robins were dying in people's front yards. No one knew why.

Rachel discovered that people had sprayed *pesticides* on their gardens. These chemicals were made to kill weeds and insects. Worms ate the plants that had been sprayed. Then robins ate the worms. Soon the robins began dying.

Rachel Carson wondered what this meant for people who ate food that had been sprayed with pesticides. She wrote a famous book called *Silent Spring*. Many people read her book and shared Carson's concern.

TAKING CARE OF OUR ENVIRONMENT

Many people are concerned that we are not taking good care of the world we live in. They are worried about how pollution hurts people and animals. They talk with our lawmakers and ask them to pass laws that are good for the environment.

Maryland has passed some laws to help clean up the air we breathe. For example, all cars must pass an *emissions* test. A machine tests cars to make sure that they do not pollute too much. Other laws tell industries what kind of emissions they can and cannot put into the air.

Governor Harry Hughes wanted to help protect the Chesapeake Bay. He got together with the states around us. They all made an agreement to protect the bay. This was an important step because pollution does not stop at our state's borders. If one state pollutes, the whole bay is harmed.

The Chesapeake Bay Foundation in Annapolis has worked for many years to teach people why it is so important to keep our water safe. It encourages our lawmakers to vote for laws that protect our environment.

▲ Photo by Brent Emil, Courtesy of U.S. Fish and Wildlife Service

In 2000, an oil pipeline burst in Maryland. Oil got into wetlands and into the Patuxent River. It got all over birds and fish. Birds cannot live with oil on their feathers. They cannot fly or get food. They get very cold. When they try to clean their feathers, they eat the poisonous oil. There are organizations that train people to clean oiled birds and other wildlife. Sometimes they can save them.

James Rouse built the town of Columbia. He wanted it to be a good place for all kinds of people to live. He wanted Columbia to offer nice homes and good schools for everyone.

▼Photos by Suzanne Chapelle

REBUILDING OUR CITIES

We know that our cities are very important. Many people live in urban areas. Many businesses are in our cities. Most theaters, concert halls, museums, and zoos are located in cities. In recent years, leaders in Maryland have been working hard to make our cities safe, attractive places.

Across Maryland, there are new downtown shopping areas, houses, and parks. Cities are trying to cut down crime. They are trying to improve the schools. Everyone wants the cities to be good places to live. It is hard work to solve all the problems.

Public Transportation

Cars pollute the air, but people who do not have cars find it hard to get to work. Everyone hates sitting in traffic jams! Running cars is expensive. The answer to these problems is good public transportation.

Maryland has several big public transportation projects. MARC trains and the Metro connect Maryland and Virginia suburbs with Washington, D.C. Baltimore's Light Rail trains go to the BWI Airport.

The more people use trains and buses, the less we have to worry about traffic jams and air pollution. More public transportation will make our cities nicer places to live.

Like many people in Maryland, the Kim family rides the new commuter trains.

Modern Maryland

How did you celebrate the year 2000? On New Year's Eve, fireworks exploded high above Baltimore Harbor.

MARYLAND IN 2000

Marylanders celebrated the beginning of the year 2000 with fireworks and parties. They looked back at the history of our state and the world. They also looked forward to our future. Some people made New Year's *resolutions* to do good things.

Each one of us is a part of history. We are all important in the history of our family, community, state, and world. When you help clean up your neighborhood, you help protect our whole environment. When you collect food for people who are hungry, you are helping solve the problem of poverty. When you welcome someone from a different place or culture, you are making the American dream become a reality. What you do today is the history of tomorrow!

Activity

How diverse is your classroom? To do this activity you will need: a large map of the world; red, blue, and green string; and pins or tacks.

1. Was anyone in your class born in a foreign country? Find the country (or countries) on the map. Stretch a piece of red string from each of the countries to Maryland. Pin each end of the string down with a tack.

2. Does anyone have a parent who was born in a foreign country? Find the countries on the map. Stretch a piece of blue string from each country to Maryland and pin it down.

3. Where do your classmates' ancestors come from? Find all the countries. With the green string, connect the countries to Maryland.

Questions for Review

1. What did the G.I. Bill do for war veterans?

2. Name two large highways built in Maryland in the 1960s.

3. What important new bridge brought lots of traffic to the Eastern Shore?

4. Name an invention that became popular after World War II.

5. In what two Asian countries did Maryland soldiers fight during the 1950s, 60s, and 70s?

6. Give one reason why some people were against the Vietnam War.

7. What kinds of discrimination did African Americans face before the Civil Rights Movement?

8. What lawyer from Maryland won a famous case about equality in the schools?

9. Who was the first African American from Maryland elected to the United States Congress?

10. List three countries from which recent immigrants have come.

Geography Tie-In

The changes that have taken place since the 1950s have had both good and bad sides. Look at the chart to see some examples.

Good	Bad
New highways make it easier to get places.	There are bad accidents because people can drive very fast.
	All the cars on the road cause air pollution.
Suburban houses are pleasant places to live. It is fun to shop at the mall.	Farms, forests, and wetlands were destroyed to build neighborhoods and parking lots.

As a class, discuss how the changes people make affect our natural areas. Discuss how much growth is too much.

Our State Government

*Representatives from all over Maryland come together
to make the laws for our state.*
(Photo by Tom Darden)

chapter 10

After America won the War for Independence, our Founding Fathers formed a new kind of goverment.

James Madison of Virginia is called the "Father of the Constitution." He provided many of the ideas that became the basic law of our country.

GOVERNMENT FOR THE NATION

On July 4, 1776, the thirteen American colonies declared their independence from England. They set up a new nation called the United States of America. They wanted their country to be a *republic*. This meant there would be no kings, queens, or princes. In the United States, the people would elect their leaders.

In the 1780s, George Washington and other leaders gathered to create their new government. First they met in Annapolis. Then the *delegates* called for a second meeting in Philadelphia. There, our Founding Fathers wrote the United States Constitution.

Writing the Constitution was a difficult job. The delegates disagreed on how strong or weak the national government should be. They argued about what powers the government should have. In the end, they were able to compromise.

Our New Constitution

The new constitution set up a *federal* system of government. This means that we have both a national government and state governments. Each has certain powers.

Our national government is made up of three branches. Here is what each branch does:

- **Legislative Branch:** This branch makes the laws. It is the United States Congress. It is made up of an upper house, called the Senate, and a lower house, called the House of Representatives. Only Congress has the power to declare war and tax the people.

- **Executive Branch:** This branch carries out the laws. It is the president of the United States and the advisors the president chooses.

- **Judicial Branch:** This branch says what the laws mean. It is the Supreme Court and lower federal courts.

The Bill of Rights

Many people liked the new Constitution. But others worried that important rights, like freedom of speech and religion, might be forgotten. They asked for a document that would clearly state the rights belonging to each American. Ten amendments were added to the Constitution. These amendments were called the Bill of Rights.

REPRESENTATIVES OF THE PEOPLE

The government of the United States is a *representative democracy*. This means that the people elect representatives to vote for them. This is like your class voting for a representative to go to a student council meeting. The student council members from all of the classes vote for certain things for the whole school.

In government, if the representatives do not vote the way the people want, then the people will vote for someone else next time. This keeps the power in the hands of the people.

The paper has yellowed and faded, but the words of the Constitution are still the basis for our government today.

Barbara Mikulski and Paul Sarbanes represent Maryland in the U.S. Senate.

Maryland's Representatives in Congress

Representatives from Maryland and all of the fifty states go to Washington, D.C., to make laws for the whole country. Two people from Maryland are elected to serve in the Senate. Eight representatives from Maryland are elected to serve in the House of Representatives. That is because Maryland is divided into eight parts, or *districts*. One representative comes from each of the districts.

Who Can Vote?

Who can vote for representatives? Who can vote for the president of the United States or the governor of Maryland? Today, anyone who is a citizen of the United States, is at least eighteen years old, and is registered (signed up) can vote.

WHAT ARE POLITICAL PARTIES?

To run for some government offices, a person must first be *nominated*, or named. Most people are nominated by one of the political parties. Political parties are groups of people who have a lot of the same ideas about government.

Most people choose either the Democratic Party or the Republican Party. Those are the two main parties in Maryland and the rest of the United States.

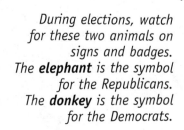

*During elections, watch for these two animals on signs and badges. The **elephant** is the symbol for the Republicans. The **donkey** is the symbol for the Democrats.*

There are also other parties, known as third parties. As another choice, some citizens do not belong to any party. They run for office or vote as independents. They do not often win elections, but they do get a chance to say what they think is important.

A person who runs for office is called a *candidate*. Candidates raise money, make posters, buy TV and radio advertising, and give speeches. At voting time, the people vote for the candidates they think will do the best job.

CAMP DAVID

Because Maryland is so close to our national capital, many federal offices are located in our state. Many people from Maryland work for the federal government.

Camp David, near Thurmont, is a retreat for the president and his guests. It is a place in the Catoctin Mountains where the president can get away from the busy crowds in Washington. The president and his family can relax there.

Camp David is a good place to play, but it is also a good place to work. Many very important meetings have been held there. During World War II, President Roosevelt and the British leader Winston Churchill held secret meetings there. Even though Churchill visited the town, the people of Thurmont kept the secret. They never said that they had seen the famous visitor until the war was over.

Before it was called Camp David, the beautiful place was called Shangri-La. President Eisenhower re-named it Camp David. He chose that name after his grandson, David Eisenhower.

President Carter invited the leaders of Egypt and Israel to Camp David. They worked out an important peace agreement that ended many years of war between Egypt and Israel.

President Kennedy walked with his son John Jr. while his daughter Caroline rode her pony "Tex."

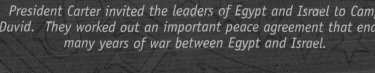

Branches of Government

Look at the giant government tree to review what you have learned about government. Study the picture to see all the interesting things that go on in each branch.

Legislative Branch

The men and women elected to make the laws are our representatives. They are also called *legislators*. On the legislative branch, find the people who are debating and giving speeches about what laws they want to be passed. Find the people who travel back and forth to the executive branch to get bills signed.

Executive Branch

The executive branch carries out the laws. The president is head of the country's executive branch. Find the reporters asking questions. Find the people trying to come in to talk with the president. Find the guard outside the room.

Judicial Branch

The courts make up the judicial branch. Courts decide what the laws mean. They try people accused of breaking a law. They work to settle problems in a peaceful way.

A *jury* is a group of people who listen to cases and decide if a person is innocent or guilty. A judge helps everyone understand the laws and gives a sentence. Find the judge, jury, and court reporter. The court reporter writes down everything that is said in court.

Constitution and Bill of Rights

Our government is based on our Constitution. It is the most important document in the whole United States. The Bill of Rights is also very important. It states that our government cannot make laws to take away our freedoms, such as freedom of speech or religion. Talk with your teacher and your class about other rights in the Bill of Rights.

Political Parties

Political parties are groups of people who share many of the same ideas about government and what it should do for the people. Find the elephant and the donkey at the base of the tree. Do you remember which parties they stand for?

Voting

The most important thing to remember about our government is that its leaders represent all of us. Find the people voting for their leaders. Then find those leaders climbing up the tree to serve in one of the branches of government.

▲ Drawing by Jon Burton

▲ Photo by Tom Darden

The laws for Maryland are made at the State House in Annapolis.

Dr. Delores Kelley is a state senator.

GOVERNMENT FOR MARYLAND

Because the fifty states of our country have different geography, people, and industries, each state has different needs and problems. Each state has a state government to meet these needs and solve these problems.

Maryland's government passes laws to help protect the Chesapeake Bay and our rivers. It operates the University of Maryland system of colleges and universities. It supports businesses across the state.

Like the national government, the state government is divided into three branches. Each branch has certain duties. That way the power is balanced. Balancing power is a very important part of our government.

▲ Photo by Suzanne Chapelle

The Maryland Adventure

Legislative Branch

In Maryland, the legislative branch is called the General Assembly. It is made up of the Senate and the House of Delegates. They make the laws for the state of Maryland.

People from all over Maryland vote for their favorite candidates. Then the people tell their representatives how they feel about problems. They write letters, call on the phone, send e-mail, or talk to representatives at their offices.

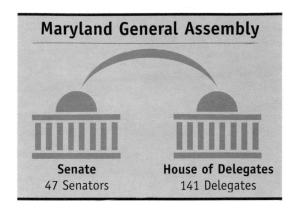

Maryland General Assembly

Senate
47 Senators

House of Delegates
141 Delegates

Executive Branch

The governor is the head of the state executive branch. The governor is elected by the people of Maryland. Here is a list of some jobs the governor does.

- Sees that state laws are carried out.
- Prepares a state budget.
- Signs *bills* into law or *vetoes* them.
- Calls the General Assembly into special extra meetings.
- Appoints people to run state programs.
- Acts as the commander in chief of the state units of the National Guard.

Many people help the governor in the executive branch. Some collect tax money. Others help people get licenses to drive cars or run businesses, inspect farm animals, work for our state parks and roads, or protect our health and environment. Many work in education.

Parris Glendening is Maryland's governor in the year 2000. Kathleen Kennedy Townshend is lieutenant governor.

Judicial Branch

The courts make up the third branch of our state government. Courts decide who is right when people disagree on what a law means. Courts also decide if a person is guilty of a crime.

The judge and often a jury listen to the reports of police officers. They listen to other people who might have been involved. After everyone has been heard, the jury must decide if the person on trial is guilty or innocent. If the person is found guilty of the crime, the judge decides how the person should be punished.

In another kind of case, a person might feel that he or she has not been treated fairly. A person might ask the courts to decide who was to blame for an accident. The court will listen to both sides and then decide on a way to settle the argument.

Robert Bell is Chief Judge of the Maryland Court of Appeals. It is the highest court in the state.

In addition to branches of government, there are levels of government. Study the chart to see how this works. What level of government does the president of the United States work under? What level of government is the mayor of your town or city? What level of government is our state's governor?

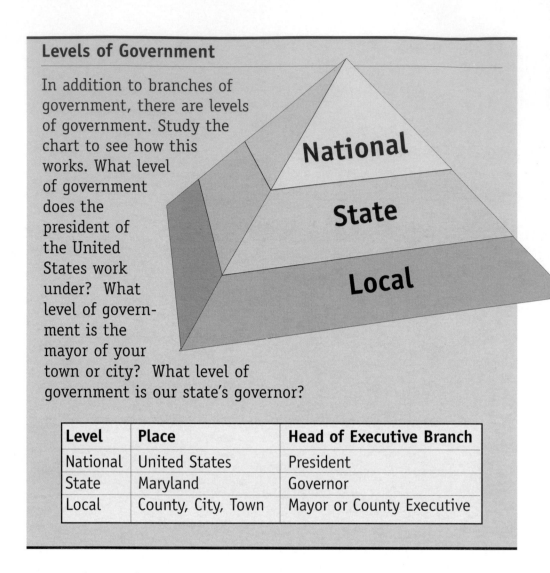

Level	Place	Head of Executive Branch
National	United States	President
State	Maryland	Governor
Local	County, City, Town	Mayor or County Executive

LOCAL GOVERNMENT

In some places in Maryland, wheat and cornfields cover the land. In other places, skyscrapers and apartment buildings are all you can see. Cities might have a very high population, with crowded roads and sidewalks. Other places are quieter, with very few people.

Because different places in our state have different needs, *local* governments are important. Local governments are governments close to home. County and city governments are both local governments.

County Government

Maryland is divided into twenty-three counties. Each county has a town that is the county seat, where the government offices are

You and your family live under the laws of the local, state, and national government.

located. (Baltimore City is not part of any county. It has its own government that does the same jobs the county governments do.)

Each county has a county executive and a council. People in each county vote for their executive and council members.

Judges and juries hear cases at the county courthouse. Births, deaths, and marriages are recorded there. If your family owns property, a map of your property is recorded in your county courthouse.

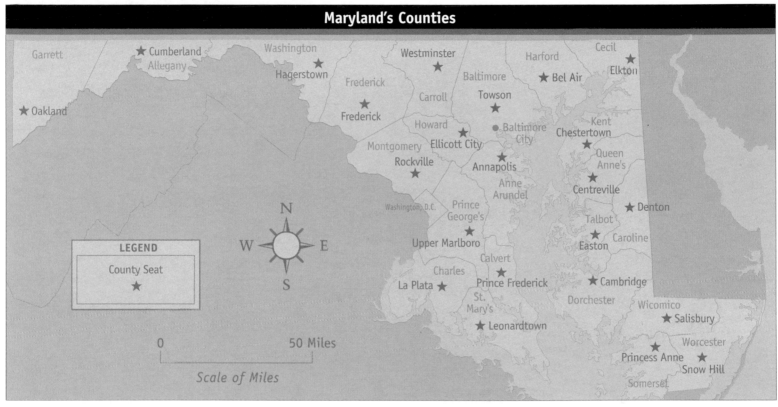

Maryland's Counties

LEGEND
County Seat
★

0   50 Miles
Scale of Miles

What county do you live in? What town is your county seat?

City Government

Another kind of local government is city government. There are different kinds of city governments. Cities are usually run by a mayor or a city manager with a city council. In Maryland, not all cities and towns have their own governments. Some are just a part of a county.

Counties and cities make rules about what kinds of buildings can be built in different regions. They make laws about speed limits on the roads. They run schools. Cities also have city courts.

Cities and counties set speed limits. What is the speed limit on the road in front of your school?

Financing the State

Where the money comes from:

Income tax
Property tax
Sales tax
License fees

Where the money goes:
Government employees
Schools
Highways
Farms
Cities
Health care
Interest on debts
Environment

What do you think**?**

Can you think of local laws, sometimes called **ordinances**, that affect you? They might have to do with speed limits, crosswalks, dog licenses, garbage pick-up, buses or taxis, or rules for your park or swimming pool.
• Why do think these laws were passed?
• Which laws do you agree with?
• Which ones would you like to change, and why?

TAXES PAY FOR SERVICES

Our state constitution gives the state, county, and city governments the power to collect taxes. Tax money pays for the services that governments provide.

Taxes come in many forms. People and businesses pay taxes on their income. When you buy new clothes or toys at stores, you pay a sales tax. Our license plate fees and highway tolls are also a kind of tax. Each county collects taxes on land, homes, and other buildings. These are called property taxes.

What is tax money used for? Taxes pay for fixing local streets and for plowing snow. Taxes pay for libraries, where you can check out books. They pay for parks, where you can play ball and have picnics. Taxes sometimes pay for the fireworks you see on the Fourth of July.

Cities and counties arrange for a clean water supply for people to use. They have your garbage picked up. If you play soccer or basketball on a local team, you may be using a city or county service. If you swim in a public pool, you are using your local government services.

One of the most important things taxes pay for is education. If you go to a public school, your school building, books, and even your teachers are paid for with tax money. If you go to a private school, your parents have to pay for these things. But the state might help pay for books for private schools.

Be a Good Citizen

Maryland is only as good as its people. That means all of the people—male and female, rich and poor, young and old—must be good citizens. They need to get involved in government and help others whenever they can.

Here are some things you can do to be a good citizen. Discuss these ideas as a class. What other things can you do? Make a list on the board.

- Obey all of your family and school rules.
- Be polite and helpful to others.
- Treat people fairly.
- Help keep your home and yard clean.
- Never litter.
- Never leave graffiti (writing on walls or buildings).
- Ask adults in your family to vote.
- Tell you representatives what you want them to do (by letter or e-mail).
- Write a letter to the editor of a newspaper. Letters from kids often get published!
- Talk with adults about what is going on in government.

1. When did our Founding Fathers declare independence from England?
2. Name the important document written by James Madison and other important leaders that is the basis for our government.
3. What are the three branches of government?
4. In the United States we elect _____ and _____ _____ to vote for us in government meetings.
5. Who can vote in the United States today? Was this always true?
6. Name the two main political parties.
7. Who is the current governor of Maryland?
8. When the governor refuses to sign a bill, he_____ it.
9. A _____ or a _____ decides if a person is guilty of a crime.
10. List three things that tax money is used for.

1. On a wall map, locate Washington, D.C. (our nation's capital), and Annapolis (our state capital). Locate your county and city or town. Then see what counties are near yours.
2. In Maryland, we are lucky. Our representatives don't have to travel very far to get to Washington, D.C. Choose two other states on the map.
   - How far do their representatives have to travel to get to Washington?
   - What are some of the ways their representatives might travel? What states might they drive through or fly over?

Making a Living in Maryland

chapter 11

Catching seafood has always been a way for people to make a living in Maryland. This man holds two of the Chesapeake Bay's finest—giant blue crabs.
(Photo by Middleton Evans)

ECONOMICS FOR EVERYONE

PEOPLE HAVE NEEDS. They also have wants. They need food, clothing, and shelter. They want things like cars, books, toys, and bicycles. These things are called *goods*, or products.

People also need medical care from doctors and nurses. They need education from teachers. They may want help repairing their washing machine or fixing a broken window. These are called *services*.

Economics is the study of how people get the goods and services that they need and want. An economic system is a way of producing and selling the goods and services people need and want.

When we are children, usually an adult takes care of meeting our needs. When we grow up, we must make a living to meet our own needs. Many adults also take care of other people—children, older relatives, and some-times friends. In this chapter, we will see how people in Maryland earn money to meet their needs.

THE FREE ENTERPRISE SYSTEM

There are many different economic systems. Different countries in the world use different systems. The United States has what is called a capitalistic or *free enterprise* system. Many Americans make their living in the free enterprise system. Here is how it works:

- People own the factories and companies that produce goods and services. The business is the property of the owner or owners.
- Owners decide what to produce and how much to charge for it. Owners decide where to do business. They decide who they want to help them. They are also in charge of selling the product.

Business owners usually hire other people, called *employees*, to work for them. The owner pays the employees a wage or a salary. Most adults in the United States are employees.

Nadine Yoritomo is a nurse. Does she provide a good or a service?

Making a Profit

How do business owners make money? Usually they sell what the workers produce. They can sell goods or services. The grocery store sells food. Dentists sell their services to fix your teeth.

A *profit* is the money a business earns after it subtracts *expenses*. People who make cars have to pay for the steel, the glass, and the tires. These are expenses. They also have to pay their employees to make cars. So, they must sell the cars for more than it costs to make them. If not, they will have a loss instead of a profit. They will soon be out of business.

People use money to buy the things they need and want. Do you earn money? Do you spend it wisely?

Supply and Demand

How do business owners decide how much to charge for their products? The selling price depends on a lot of things. The business has to make a profit. Sometimes the price also depends on how much of something there is. If a toy becomes so popular that a company cannot make enough for everyone who wants it, the company can sell the toy for a higher price. People will be willing to pay more to get it. This is called the rule of *supply and demand*.

Sometimes a company has to lower its prices. Maybe a company makes bicycles and tries to sell them at a certain price, but people don't buy very many of them. So the company has a lot of extra bicycles sitting around. They might lower the price to get people to buy them. Or maybe there are two companies that make bicycles. One of the companies might lower its price to get people to buy from it instead of from the other company.

Sometimes there is only one company that produces a certain product. Then the owners can charge about whatever price they want. If buyers want that product or service, they will have to pay whatever price the company charges.

If a store has too many basketballs, the balls might go on sale.

MARYLAND ENTREPRENEURS

Many people in Maryland are *entrepreneurs*. An entrepreneur is someone who has an idea and the courage to start a business. Entrepreneurs work for themselves. Sometimes the whole family helps with the business. Even children often help with the family business. Let's meet some of Maryland's entrepreneurs.

Sharon Tufaro and Nancy Cusack started a toy store.

Nancy Cusack and Sharon Tufaro

Nancy Cusack and Sharon Tufaro own a toy store named Shananigans. They sell wonderful toys for boys and girls.

Nancy and Sharon have two part-time employees, but they do most of the work themselves. They buy the toys from the companies that make them. They work in the store selling the toys. They take out the trash, dust the shelves, pay the bills, and make the phone calls. If Nancy is sick or wants to go on vacation, Sharon has to be there to open the store. You can see that it is a lot of work to own your own business.

Tom Washburn

Tom Washburn opened an ice cream parlor. He named it Moxley's, after his dog. He offers cones, milkshakes, sundaes, and ice cream cakes.

Tom makes his ice cream right at Moxley's. He buys strawberries and peaches from local farmers. He also buys cocoa, vanilla, and other flavors that are not produced in Maryland. He has a big machine that mixes and freezes the ice cream. Then Tom puts it into the blast freezer. The next day, the ice cream is ready.

Tom and his wife Nettie have two sons. Ty is four years old and Will is two. When Ty's nursery school class has a party, Tom donates ice cream. Tom also gives ice cream to school classes that visit Moxley's. He gives ice cream coupons to local charities and churches.

Tom Washburn serves his customers "Baltimore's best" homemade ice cream.

The Maryland Adventure

William Coulbourne

William Coulbourne and his partner, Frederick Jewett, started a seafood company 100 years ago in St. Michaels. As young men, they had both worked as oyster shuckers. Oyster shuckers cut open the thick shells and take out the oysters.

To start their own oyster company, the partners borrowed money to buy equipment. They bought oysters from local watermen. They hired employees to shuck and can the oysters. Then they sold the cans to stores and restaurants along the East Coast.

The company was a success! It grew and grew. Soon the company was canning crab meat, too. Coulbourne and Jewett became the largest employer in St. Michaels. The two entrepreneurs retired in the 1940s. They could live well because their business had been successful.

Dr. Jane Brunt

Dr. Jane Brunt is a *veterinarian*, or a doctor for animals. Her business is called the Cat Hospital at Towson. Its nickname is CHAT, the French word for "cat." Dr. Brunt was the first veterinarian in Maryland to specialize in treating cats.

Dr. Brunt and her employees take x-rays and set broken legs. They perform surgery, do physicals, and give dental care. CHAT also provides a place for cats to stay when their families go out of town.

Dr. Brunt had to buy the building where her office is and all her equipment. She has to pay for the heat, electric power, and water. She pays a staff that includes three other veterinarians, five technicians, and twenty-three other people who help take care of the animals, keep records, answer the phones, and check in the patients. The fees CHAT charges cover all these expenses.

William Coulbourne and his partner started a seafood company.

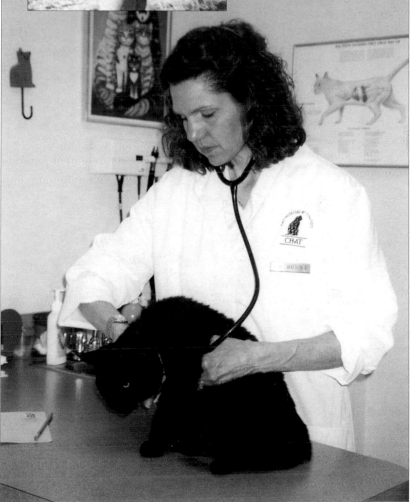

Dr. Brunt listens to "Tommy's" heartbeat.

Making a Living in Maryland

Natural Resources

If you are making chairs, you might use wood. If you are making teddy bears, you may need cotton to stuff them. Cotton and wood are both natural resources that grow on the land. Machines need energy. This energy can come from coal, oil, the sun, and even the wind. They are natural resources, too.

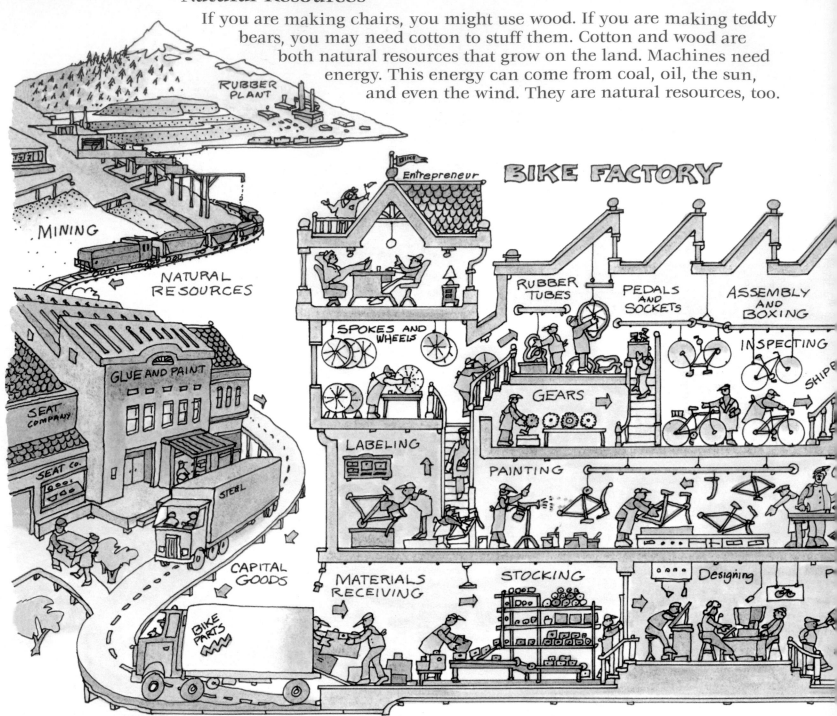

Capital Resources

When you use things that are already made to make something else, you are using capital goods. A carpenter doesn't make his own hammer—he just uses it to build a house. The hammer and nails a carpenter uses are capital goods. The money you need to start and run a business is also called capital.

Entrepreneurship

Entrepreneurship is owning and running a business. It often starts with an idea. The person must be willing to take a risk to make the idea work. Entrepreneurs use natural resources, human resources, and capital goods to make money.

Factors of Production

There are things that must come together before something is sold as a good or service. These things are called factors of production. They are natural, human, and capital resources.

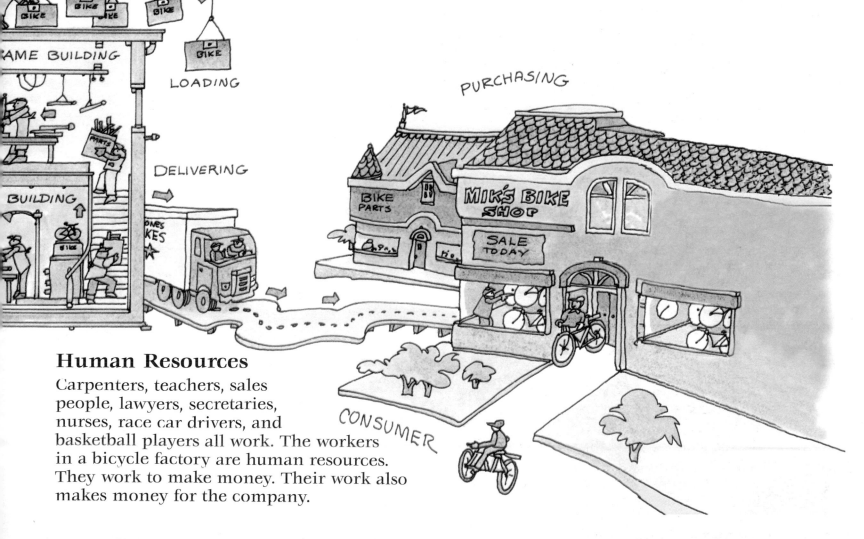

Human Resources

Carpenters, teachers, sales people, lawyers, secretaries, nurses, race car drivers, and basketball players all work. The workers in a bicycle factory are human resources. They work to make money. Their work also makes money for the company.

CONSUMERS BUY GOODS AND SERVICES

People are workers. They are also consumers. A consumer is a person who buys goods and services. Anyone who spends money is a consumer. Are you a consumer? What kinds of things do you buy with your money?

People want to spend their money wisely. They compare different brands and prices at different stores. They also want to make sure that what they buy is really what they want.

Does seeing this ad for Wild Things Sunglasses make you want to buy a pair?

Advertising

Businesses use advertising to get consumers to buy their products and services. Advertising may be on the radio, on TV, on the Internet, or in newspapers and magazines. You see and hear it everywhere.

Advertising is important to business and important to the people who work for the company. Remember, a business has to make a profit. If the consumers don't know about a product, will they buy it?

Being a wise consumer means understanding how advertising works. Have you ever bought something because the advertisements made it seem exciting, then you found out it wasn't? Do you always believe everything a commercial says?

Methods Used in Advertising

1. **Color and excitement.** The ad is bright and colorful so people will notice it. The product seems fun and exciting.

2. **Repetition.** The ad says a name or slogan over and over.

3. **Social appeal.** The ad suggests that if you use a certain product you will look nice and have a lot of friends.

4. **Humor.** People like and remember things that are funny.

5. **Music.** People remember short tunes and jingles.

Major industries like Bethlehem Steel are next to the bay. Ships, trains, and trucks can all come directly to the plant.

TRANSPORTATION AND TRADE

Transportation of natural resources and finished products is very important for business. Without good transportation, business would almost stop.

Can you think of some things that you consume that come from far away? Look and see where your television was made. Find out where chocolate comes from. How do you think these things get to Maryland?

Airports: Baltimore-Washington International Airport serves the entire state. In addition to passengers, lots of *freight* travels in and out of BWI. We put goods on airplanes to go to all parts of the world.

Railroads: Since the B&O Railroad was built, trains have been important to our state's economy. Today, the CSX Corporation runs the largest freight rail system in Maryland.

Trains bring goods into Maryland and take natural resources, farm products, and manufactured items out of the state.

Roads and Highways: Roads have been important to Maryland since the early days of settlement. Today, major interstates such as I-95, I-70, and I-68 link Maryland to the rest of the nation.

Waterways: The Chesapeake Bay provided a way for the first settlers to come to Maryland. The bay is just as important to the people of Maryland today. Ships sail up and down the bay, to and from the Atlantic Ocean. Most are sailing to Baltimore, our state's largest port. Trains and trucks connect the port to other parts of our state and nation.

Large ships like this one sail up the Chesapeake Bay into the port of Baltimore.

MARYLAND AT WORK

When Maryland went from a colony to a state, most people farmed. In the 1800s, manufacturing and the seafood business became very important. Farming, providing seafood, and manufacturing are still very important here. But today most people work in service jobs. They are nurses, engineers, drivers, and teachers.

Many Marylanders work in retail stores or for the government. Can you name someone who works in a store? Do you know someone who works for the national, state, or local government? What does he or she do?

High-Tech Industries

New high-tech industries are very important in our state's economy. Maryland companies develop parts and programs for computers. Scientists do research to try to improve technology. *Telecommunications* companies also do business in Maryland. They work on better ways for people to communicate by phone and computer. Products for use in space are also being developed.

Science and Medicine

Maryland is known as a center of scientific and medical research. The Johns Hopkins Hospital in Baltimore is known around the world for medical research and treatment. The National Library of Medicine in Montgomery County is the largest in the world.

The Catch of the Day

All of the waterways around Maryland produce seafood. Crabs, clams, oysters, and fish are shipped to all parts of the U.S. and to countries around the world. Every year, the seafood industry contributes over $400 million to Maryland's economy.

From the Farm to Your Table

Maryland is lucky to have good fertile farmland. We can grow a lot of our own food. We also *export* some of our farm products.

Maryland farmers grow a lot of soybeans, corn, and wheat. They grow vegetables such as tomatoes, squash, and beans. They grow fruits such as peaches and watermelons. Dairy farms produce milk and cream.

BP Solarex in Frederick makes and sells solar power systems. Solar power is energy from the sun. The panels on the roof of their building collect the sun's energy.

Many farmers raise chickens in poultry houses.

The Norman family grows **organic** vegetables and herbs. They sell them at a local farmers' market.

Photo by Suzanne Chapelle

Enjoy Maryland!

When people visit Maryland, they can see history come alive in St. Mary's City, swim at the beach in Ocean City, watch a dolphin show at the National Aquarium in Baltimore, or cheer at a Baltimore Orioles game. This is all part of *tourism*—a major industry in Maryland.

People who visit Maryland spend money on transportation, hotels, food, entertainment, and recreation. All of these things make money for the businesses and workers of Maryland.

Ocean City's beaches and boardwalk draw crowds all summer long, year after year.

Maryland Companies	
Black Entertainment TV	cable television shows
Celera Genomics	medical research
Lockheed Martin	global telecommunications, satellites, defense products
Marriott International	hotels, senior living services, food distribution
McCormick and Company	herbs and spices

Non-Profit Organizations

A *non-profit* organization hires people to help make the world a better place. The organization pays its employees, but it does not make a profit. Any money it makes goes to programs that help people.

Kweisi Mfume runs the NAACP.

Non-Profit Groups	
Abell Foundation	education and city life
Annie E. Casey Foundation	children and families
Goodwill Industries International, Inc.	job training
National Association for the Advancement of Colored People (NAACP)	civil rights

SHARING OUR MONEY

In an earlier chapter, you read about philanthropists who lived 100 years ago. Do you remember what a philanthropist does? A philanthropist shares his or her wealth to help other people.

There are many philanthropists in Maryland today. Businessman Joseph Meyerhoff and other members of his family gave a lot of money to the Baltimore Symphony Orchestra so everyone can enjoy wonderful music. Baseball player Eddie Murray gave money for the Carrie Murray Nature Center, where children and adults from the city can spend time outside learning about nature.

Volunteering—Philanthropy for Everyone

You don't have to be wealthy to help make the world a better place. People can give their time by volunteering.

Many businesses encourage their employees to volunteer in their communities. Schools in Maryland encourage students to volunteer. Many retired people volunteer because they have more time than they did when they were working. Have you ever been a volunteer? What did you do?

What do you think**?**

Someday you will be a grownup. If you could choose any job in the world, what would it be? Would your job be in farming, manufacturing, or service? Or would you choose to work on the water?

Most jobs not only give the worker a salary but help other people meet needs or wants. Think of ways in which your job might help people.

This man volunteers to work with children.

Goods and Services

Goods are things that are made in factories, workshops, or even at home. They are then sold for money. Shoes, pencils, televisions, and dog collars are all goods. People make money by making and selling goods.

Services are things that people do for other people. Dentists, truck drivers, umpires, coaches, and teachers provide services. People earn money by providing services.

On a separate piece of paper, number from one to twelve. Write "G" for goods or "S" for services for each job listed below.

1. Fixes the plumbing
2. Collects the garbage
3. Teaches students
4. Manufactures paint
5. Makes engines for cars
6. Repairs cars
7. Delivers cheese to grocery stores
8. Makes telephones
9. Repairs telephones
10. Manufactures light bulbs
11. Takes care of the cat while you're away
12. What you would like to do when you grow up

1. What economic system is used the the U.S.?
2. If you work for someone else you are an _____.
3. What is a profit?
4. What is supply and demand?
5. What is an entrepreneur?
6. What are the four factors of production?
7. A person who buys things is called a _____.
8. List two types of transportation and tell why each is important to Maryland's businesses.
9. What are four large industries in Maryland today?
10. List at least three jobs that provide services. Tell why they are services, not goods.
11. Name four food products that come from Maryland.
12. How do tourists help make money for Maryland?
13. What is a non-profit organization? Give two examples in Maryland.

Geography Tie-In

Have a class brainstorming session about how geography affects businesses. Choose two different businesses. Then you and your classmates say how the business is affected by the land (is it flat or hilly, on the coast or inland). Discuss available transportation networks, natural resources, human resources (workers), and how the business might affect the environment.

GLOSSARY

The terms are defined according to their use in the chapters of this textbook. Each word appears in bold italic print the first time it occurs in the book.

abolitionist: a person who wanted to end slavery

ally: a country that helps another country protect itself

almanac: a reference book with lists and charts of facts in certain subjects

amendment: a change or addition to a constitution

ammunition: bullets and other explosives for war

ancestor: a relative who lived before you

anthem: a song of praise to a country or cause

archaeologist: a scientist who learns about ancient people by studying the things they left behind

artifact: an object made by people long ago

assassinate: to murder by sudden attack

atlatl: a tool that helped early people throw a spear

atom: a tiny particle that can produce nuclear energy

barracks: buildings for lodging soldiers

bill: a written idea for a law

biology: the study of living things

border state: in Civil War times, a state located between the northern and southern states (They did not secede but still had slaves.)

candidate: a person who tries to get elected to office

century: a period of 100 years

civil rights: the rights that belong to every citizen

colony: a settlement under the control of another nation

communist: a system in which the government—not the people—owns the businesses and means of production

compromise: an agreement reached when each side gives up part of its demands

concentration camp: a horrible prison camp for Germany's prisoners during World War II

Confederacy: the group of southern states that tried to start their own country during the Civil War

congregation: a group of people who meet to worship together

conquer: to win or overthrow

consumer: someone who buys things

cooperate: to work together

council: a group of people who meet to talk about something important

debt: money owed

delegate: someone chosen to speak or act for a group of people

dense: crowded or thickly settled

department store: a large store with different departments such as clothing, home products, toys, jewelry, etc.

depression: a time when there are very few jobs and people are very poor

determined: convinced that you can do something

dictator: a ruler with all the power

discrimination: treating people unfairly because they are different in some way

district: part of a larger place

diverse: having differences, such as people from different cultures or backgrounds

drought: a long period of dry weather

economics: the study of how people use their resources to make, sell, buy, and use goods and services

economy: the way people use their resources to make, sell, buy, and use goods and services

ecosystem: a community of living things that interact and depend upon each other

emancipation: freedom or release from slavery

emissions: particles put into the air

empire: a group of countries or territories that are controlled by one ruler

employee: a person who works for a company or for someone else for wages

endangered: in danger of disappearing

entrepreneur: a person who has an idea and the courage to start a business

expense: money spent in order to make a good or provide a service

export: to send to other countries for sale

extinct: no longer existing on earth

fall line: an imaginary line made by connecting the first waterfall of each river

federal: having to do with the government of the whole country—state and national

fertile: allowing lots of things to grow well

fertilize: to add material to the soil so crops will grow better

fossil: an imprint or actual remains of a plant or animal in rock

free enterprise: a system where the people, not the government, run and own the businesses

freight: a load of goods to be transported; cargo

generator: a machine that makes electricity

gentry: the upper class

geography: the study of the earth and the people, animals, and plants living on it

ghetto: a small crowded part of a city where the poor often live

girdling: cutting into the layers of a tree in order to kill the tree

glacier: a large mass of ice built up over a long period of time

good: a product that is made, bought, and sold

gourd: a type of squash that is dried and used for bowls, ornaments, or rattles

grant: to give permission to settle on a piece of land

holocaust: destruction or devastation; the killing of European Jews and others in Nazi concentration camps during World War II

hunter-gatherer: a person who hunts animals and gathers wild foods in order to survive

ideal: an idea of what is perfect; a goal; a standard of excellence

immigrant: a person who moves into a new country to live

impel: to urge into action

import: to bring in from another place

indentured servant: a person who worked for another person for a period of time in order to pay back a debt

independence: freedom from another country's control or rule

Industrial Revolution: a change from producing things by hand to using machines

industry: manufacturing; businesses, crafts, and arts

ironworks: a mill or factory in which iron or steel is made

jury: a group of people who listen to a case and decide if a person is innocent or guilty of breaking the law

kerosene: an oil used for fuel

legislator: a person elected to make the laws

lifestyle: a way of life

local: close to home; nearby

Loyalist: a person who was faithful to the king

lynch: to kill by mob violence, usually hanging

mass production: making many things at once, usually with machines

midden: an ancient trash pile

migrant: a person who moves from place to place in order to find work

migrate: to move from place to place

military: having to do with the armed forces

militia: a part of the army to be used in local emergencies

miniature: a small version of something

native: coming from a certain place naturally

nominate: to name or choose as a candidate

non-profit: not done to make money

official: authorized; allowed by the law

ordain: to let into the ministry or priesthood

ordinance: a local law

organic: grown without pesticides or other harmful chemicals

outlaw: to make illegal

overseer: a person who has the job of watching others to make sure they work

palisade: a high fence for protection

Patriot: a person who wanted the thirteen colonies to be free of the rule of England; someone who loves his or her country

peninsula: a piece of land that sticks out into the water and has water on three sides

pesticide: a chemical used to kill insects

petroglyph: designs the American Indians carved into rocks on the sides of cliffs or hills

philanthropist: someone who gives away money to help others

plantation: a large farming estate

politics: the activities of the government

powwow: an American Indian meeting or ceremony

predator: an animal that lives by hunting other animals

privateer: a sailor on a ship that has permission to attack enemy ships

profit: the money left after expenses are paid

Progressive: a person who wanted the government to solve social problems and help the poor

prohibit: to forbid

proprietor: the person in charge; an owner, ruler, or governor

protest: to complain against an idea or action; to speak out against something

ration: a little bit of something that has to be divided among many people

raw materials: materials used to make something else

rebellion: a fight against those in power

rebellious: anxious to fight against those in power

reliable: able to depend on

renaissance: a re-birth or new beginning

replica: a copy of something

representative: someone elected to vote for other people

representative democracy: a type of government in which the people choose representatives to vote and make the laws for them

republic: a government in which the people have the power to vote and where there is usually a president

resist: to fight against

resolution: a goal; a promise to yourself

retreat: to withdraw or move back

revolution: to overthrow a government; a big change in the way things are done

saint: a holy or honored person

sapling: a young tree

satellite: a machine in space that orbits stars and planets

secede: to leave a country to form another country

segregate: to separate by race

service: (in economics) something done for another person for money

silt: soil particles floating in rivers, ponds, or lakes

sinew: a tendon or tissue from inside an animal

slave: a person who is forced to work for someone else without pay

stock: money invested in a business

suburb: an area with houses and streets just outside of a city

supply and demand: a rule in economics that says that how much there is of something affects how much it will cost

survey: to examine and measure the land

tax: to force the people to pay money to the government

telecommunications: communication at a distance, as with telephone or radio

temperate: not too hot and not too cold; not extreme

temporary: lasting only for a short time

tolerate: to accept

tourism: when people tour or visit places for pleasure

traditional: handed down from parents to children in the same way as things were done in the past

treason: acting against the government by spying or planning to overthrow it

tributary: a small river that flows into a larger river or body of water

union: a group of workers who form an organization to get more money and better working conditions

Union: another word for the United States; the northern states during the Civil War

vaccine: a shot; medicine injected into a person to prevent a disease

veteran: a person who has served in the armed forces

veterinarian: a doctor for animals

veto: to strike down or prohibit

wampum: American Indian beadwork made from tiny shells

weir: a fence put in a waterway for catching fish

INDEX

CREDITS

DRAWINGS

Burton, Jon 91, 108, 178-179, 192-193

Cornia, Ray 134, 159

Rasmussen, Gary state symbols pages, 12, 27, 28, 32 (bottom), 33 (bottom), 34, 35, 36, 37, 39, 42, 43, 47, 59, 72 (map)

MAPS by Robert Holman

PHOTOGRAPHS

Alan Mason Cheney Medical Archives, Johns Hopkins Medical Institutions 164 (bottom)

Albin O. Kuhn Library, University of Maryland, Baltimore City, Edward O. Bafford Collection 128 (left)

Archive Photos, 161

B&O Railroad Museum 99

BP Solarex 196

Baker, Will: Courtesy of the Chesapeake Bay Foundation 9 (right)

Barrow, Scott 163 (bottom)

Bell, Lance: Courtesy of ADD, Inc. contents pages (top left), 2-3, 25

C&O Canal Museum 87 (bottom), 100

Chapelle, Suzanne 14 (top), 24 (right), 169, 180 (left), 188, 190, 191 (bottom), 196 (bottom) **Courtesy of the Irvine Natural Science Center** 32 (bottom), 40, 43, 44

Chesapeake Bay Foundation 9 (left), 29

Colonial Williamsburg contents pages (third from top left), 50-51

Crossman, Jean: Courtesy of the Amherst History Museum 80 (bottom)

Darden, Tom contents page (second from bottom right), 172-173, 180 (top), 181 (top right)

Emil, Brent: Courtesy of the U.S. Fish and Wildlife Service 168 (bottom)

Enoch Pratt Free Library 102, 114 (bottom), 125 (bottom right), 137 (bottom), 138 (bottom), 143 (top)

Evans, Middleton contents pages (third from top right and third from bottom right), 10-11, 12, 16, 17, 19 (top left, top center, top right), 20, 23 (top), 57 (top), 64 (top left), 156-157, 157 (bottom right), 160 (top), 164 (top), 186-187, 195

Fisk University Archives 103 (bottom right)

Franklin Delano Roosevelt Presidential Library 149

George Eastman House 131, 135 (bottom right)

Giordano, Victor 23 (bottom), 24 (left)

Grall, George: Courtesy of the National Aquarium, Baltimore 8, 13

Harrison, Keith 19 (bottom)

Harvey, Lamont 191 (top)

Huta, Yuri 18

Instructional Resources Corporation: The History of Maryland Slide Collection contents pages (second from top right), 21, 57 (bottom), 64 (bottom), 66, 70 (bottom left, bottom right), 71 (bottom left, bottom right), 73 (top), 74 (bottom), 79 (top right), 81, 83 (both), 94, 98 (both), 101, 104 (both), 106 (bottom right), 107 (bottom left), 109 (bottom), 113, 118 (both), 121 (bottom), 126 (bottom left), 127, 128 (bottom), 132 (top), 135 (top left), 136 (left), 140-141, 141 (bottom center), 142, 146 (right), 147, 150, 153 (top right, bottom), 158, 160 (left), 163 (top)

Irvine Natural Science Center 32 (bottom), 40, 43, 44, 198

Jimmy Carter Library 177 (left)

John Fitzgerald Kennedy Library 177 (right)

Johns Hopkins University, Ferdinand Hamburger Archives 138 (top)

Library of Congress 90, 162 (left)

Maryland Historical Society contents page (second to bottom left), 51 (bottom center), 53 (center), 54, 55, 65, 79 (bottom left), 80 (top), 86-87, 86 (bottom right), 88, 92, 94 (top), 95 (right), 96, 110 (bottom), 117 (bottom), 123, 152 (both)

Maryland Office of Tourism 4, 6, 14 (bottom), 33 (bottom), 48 (left), 196 (center)

Maryland State Archives 58 (left), 61 (bottom), 135 (top right), 181 (bottom), 197 (bottom)

Mayer, Francis Blackwell 75

McKeldin Library, University of Maryland, College Park, Special Collections 109 (top)

Montgomery County Historical Society contents pages (top right), 124-125, 126 (bottom), 136 (top)

NASA 157 (bottom center), 165

New Jersey Newsphotos 157 (bottom left), 162 (center)

North Wind Picture Archives contents pages (second and fourth from top left), 32-33, 41 (center), 52, 60, 63 (bottom), 70-71, 77 (top), 93 (bottom)

Ocean City Public Relations Office 197 (top)

Office of Archaeology, Maryland Department of Housing and Community Development 36

Office of Senator Barbara Mikulski 176 (top left)

Office of Senator Paul Sarbanes 176 (bottom left)

Paul, Gregory: Courtesy of the Maryland Science Center 15

Rachel Carson History Project 168 (left)

Rouse Company, The 169

St. Mary's City Commission 56

Star-Spangled Banner Flag House 86 (bottom left), 95

Talbot County Historical Society 62 (bottom)

Till, Tom contents page (bottom left), 106-107

U.S. Fish and Wildlife Service 41 (bottom), 168 (bottom)

Warren, M. E., Courtesy of Instructional Resources Corporation: The History of Maryland Slide Collection 66, 160 (left)

Warren, Mame, Courtesy of Instructional Resources Corporation: The History of Maryland Slide Collection 21

Washington County Free Library 134 (center)

White House, The 177 (background)

All photographs not listed are from the author's collection or the collection of Gibbs Smith, Publisher.